All the Blocks Are Geese

Flying Geese—The Fast Way

Mary Sue Suit

That Patchwork Place®

DEDICATION

To Bill for all his patience and support.

Credits

Editor-in-Chief . . . . Barbara Weiland
Technical Editor . . . . Susan I. Jones
Managing Editor . . . . Greg Sharp
Copy Editor . . . . Liz McGehee
Proofreader . . . . Tina Cook
Cover Design . . . . Judy Petry
Text Design . . . . Karin LaFramboise
Typesetting . . . . Karin LaFramboise
Photography . . . . Brent Kane
Illustration and Graphics . . . . Laurel Strand

All the Blocks Are Geese©
©1994 by Mary Sue Suit

That Patchwork Place, Inc.,
PO Box 118, Bothell, WA 98041-0118
USA

Printed in Hong Kong
99 98 97 96 95 94   6 5 4 3 2

Library of Congress Cataloging-in-Publication Data
Suit, Mary Sue,
    All the blocks are geese / Mary Sue Suit :
      (photography, Brent Kane : illustration and
      graphics, Laurel Strand).
      p.   cm.
    ISBN 1-56477-049-4 :
    1. Patchwork—Patterns. 2. Quilting—Patterns.
    3. Geese in art.
  I. Title.
TT835.S8   1994
746.9'7—dc20   93-33692
                            CIP

ACKNOWLEDGMENTS

Special thanks are due to all the friends whose generous help made this book possible.

To Dorothy Bull for the extra push, the computer access, and the shared works;

To Louise Krutsinger, Sue Lurz, and the members of the Yellowstone Valley Quilters' Guild for being willing guinea pigs;

To those listed below, who on very short notice, learned the technique and made a wonderful variety of quilts to share with everyone:

    Lyn Banks
    Dorothy Bull
    Pegee Haman
    Judy Harris
    Margie Hay
    Mary Lucas
    Yvonne Morrissey
    Barbara Olsen
    Mary Ellen Reynolds
    Karen Walker

To new friends at That Patchwork Place who took a chance on me. Thanks to Susan Jones, who made my work look so good.

CONTENTS

Introduction 4
How to Use This Book 5
General Directions 6
    Tools and Materials 6
    Fabrics 6
    Flying-Geese-the-Fast-Way 8
    Square Size Table for Geese Segments 11
Flights of Fancy 12
    Traditional Flying Geese 13
    Geese and Squares 16
    Flights-of-Fancy Garments 18
All the Blocks Are Geese Sampler 20
    Blocks 21
        Dutchman's Puzzle 21
        Seesaw 21
        Next-Door Neighbor 22
        King's Crown 24
        Wild Goose Chase 24
        Aunt Sukey's Choice 25
        The Cypress 26
        Capital T 27
        Evening Star 28
        Stars and Squares 29
        Free Trade 29
        Crown and Star 31
    Quilt Assembly and Finishing 32
Two-Block Quilts 35
    Spring Mosaic 35
    Neon Desert 41
Diamond Quilts 46
    Diamond X 46
Gallery of Quilts 49
Repeat-Block Quilts 65
    Aunt Sukey's Choice 65
Borders 69
    Traditional 70
    End-to-End 70
Block Glossary 71
    Grid Formulas 71
    Blocks 72
Finishing Your Quilt 77

Introduction

It seems that every quilter has at least one quilt being pieced, one in the process of being quilted, and innumerable quilts in mind, waiting to be "hatched." The most impatient of our breed have devised quick-piecing methods of block construction, allowing the maximum number of ideas to take shape in fabric. I count myself among the most impatient.

When I was young and foolish, I felt everything must be hand pieced or not pieced at all. Fortunately, I outgrew this philosophy. While hand piecing has its place, speed machine piecing is more suited to my life-style. The need for quilts that could be used and loved to pieces loomed large as my quilting passion grew along with my children. Over the years, this attitude has led me to learn and devise a great many quick tricks. My compulsion to create became an effort to balance hard use and the time invested. Out of my balancing act has come this technique for quick-piecing Flying Geese and the happy realization that between the covers of this book, "All the Blocks Are Geese."

I have always tried to be as accurate as possible, even in my haste to create. The technique for making Flying-Geese-the-Fast-Way allows me to piece a large variety of blocks in the least amount of time, with the most accurate results.

Every new trick takes some practice. The projects in this book take you step by step through the Flying-Geese-the-Fast-Way technique and help you apply it to blocks ranging from simple to complex. The sewing required is easy! You just sew straight seams.

The sampler quilt in this book was designed so you can sew a beautiful and accurately pieced quilt top in very little time. I won't promise you a completed quilt top in an afternoon, but I will promise a vast savings of time. Because "everything is relative," the amount of time you save is in proportion to the time needed to do the job the old way.

I am a great believer in the old "If at first you don't succeed …" adage, and there have been a great many "try, try again" projects on the road to this collection of tricks. The secret to any success I have had in quick-piecing is the secret for everyone else as well—"try, try again." As adults, we encourage our children or others to try again but are quick to give up on our own projects. If we allow imperfection on a first try in others, we should be as forgiving with ourselves. Remember, don't be too hard on yourself. Don't compare youself to those around you. Use your own improvement as a guide to determine your success. Above all, enjoy yourself.

How to Use This Book

It is my objective to teach a new quick-piecing technique along with design options for Flying Geese blocks. You will learn how to piece four Flying Geese segments at once from two squares of fabric. General directions are given first, followed by specific directions for two practice projects.

The chapter containing instructions for the All the Blocks Are Geese Sampler quilt shows how to apply this new technique to traditional block patterns that contain Flying Geese sections. The chapters that follow include quilts made up of repeat blocks, two-block quilts, and a diamond block pattern. Directions for some border treatments using Flying Geese segments are also given. A glossary of pieced blocks, using the techniques outlined in the sampler section, is included, too. The best way to use this book is to learn the technique, step by step, and practice it by making one of the small projects. The most important aspect of the technique is repetition and, in turn, repetition is the best way to master it.

The quilts in this book are basic patterns with straight-seam construction. They are intended to make your work the best in the shortest time possible. I hope this book will become a source of inspiration and a resource to turn your inspiration into a reality.

General Directions

Part of the beauty of this technique is that it does not require any special equipment other than what is considered basic to the quilting process. Fabric squares are the basic piecing unit, making it ideal for use with small pieces of fabric or scraps.

TOOLS AND MATERIALS

Other than your sewing machine, thread, and scissors, you will need a rotary cutter, cutting mat, and a ruler with markings in ¼" increments. These tools are an investment, and basic to quick machine piecing and quilting in general.

Rulers

I use a marked square for cutting the original squares and trimming the Flying Geese segments. The easiest square to use has a marked diagonal line with graduated squares marked along the diagonal. The Bias Square® from That Patchwork Place works best, especially to trim the geese. Occasionally, you might need to cut a square larger than 8". A wide ruler can be used as long as it has ¼" markings. These are essential for accurate trimming. It is best if these markings form a complete ¼" grid across the entire ruler. There are several squares and rulers on the market, so if you are buying one for the first time, choose a ruler with the necessary ¼" markings that you find easy to read.

Rotary Cutter and Mat

If you are purchasing your first rotary cutter, I suggest you buy the large size. I know more than one quilter who bought the small one first and now owns one of each. It is wise to purchase the cutter at a quilt shop or store where one of the staff members can give you a lesson on how to use it. You will also need a self-healing rotary-cutting mat. I would not buy one smaller than 18" x 24".

If you are using a rotary cutter for the first time, please be careful. Remember, the blade is extremely sharp. If your rotary cutter does not close automatically, train yourself to cover the blade after every cut. Never put it down with the blade exposed, and make sure it is covered if you are using it around others while "talking with your hands." When you place your hand on the ruler to hold it in position, make sure your fingers do not hang over the edge into the path of the cutter. I had six stitches in my left index finger because I made just such an oversight. When asked if I cut myself washing dishes, I smiled and said, "Nothing so mundane." I was using the cutter again before the stitches even came out.

Iron

Last, but not least, you need a good-quality steam iron to press your seams. It took me years, but I have finally grown into pressing. Pressing is a must for accurate piecing and trimming.

In addition to these basic tools, you will need fabric (as discussed below), plus a sense of adventure and a positive "I can do it!" attitude.

FABRICS

In quilting, 100% prewashed cotton is preferred. The techniques in this book are well suited to using up scraps and small amounts of yardage. You can make excellent use of that scrap pile (mine never makes it to a bag), or use a planned assortment of fabrics. For your first project, I suggest using fabrics that you like but not the pride of your collection. Use that for your second project, after you have mastered the technique.

What we see in a quilt is determined by contrast. First, assign the color values in the Flying Geese segment by placing the light, medium, and dark fabrics in the quilt block. Each Flying Geese segment consists of two areas: a large triangle that is the goose and two small triangles of sky.

Because the eye sees high contrast easily, the Flying Geese are best defined by using lights and darks together. Traditionally, the geese are dark and the sky is light, but you can choose light geese and dark sky if you wish.

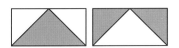

Once you have decided on the placement of lights and darks, choose your colors. Here is where raiding a scrap pile or collection can be fun. Simply go through your scraps and cut a square the correct size from each piece, matching the values and colors you chose for your Flying Geese. Do the same for the sky, or use just one fabric for the sky pieces. Selecting fabrics in this manner gives your quilt a definite scrappy appearance. You can also use specially selected fabrics and a planned placement for each fabric within your project. It's nice to have so many choices!

To recap your fabric selections: First, decide on the value placement in the Flying Geese segment. Second, choose your colors. Third, decide if your quilt project will be scrappy or planned. I have found that making these decisions is enough to get started. Worry about setting the project together after you have pieced the Flying Geese segments. I inevitably find that if I plan an entire project at once, no matter how sure I am of the outcome, I change something along the way.

Organizing Your Fabrics

Most people suffering from the quilt bug have accumulated an extensive fabric collection. I am no exception. One of the best tricks I have learned is how to sort and store my collection in an easy, inexpensive way. Like many valuable tricks, I stumbled upon this idea quite by accident. When faced with a household move, I decided the time had come to sort and organize my fabrics. I found the best source of sturdy boxes was the local liquor store. My first intent was simply to fill each box with a different color of fabric. The fact that the cardboard cubbyholes used to separate the bottles were still in the boxes was a wonderful happenstance. I had picked boxes that originally contained large bottles, giving me beautiful 6"–8" sections to fill with my small pieces of yardage. First, I divided the fabric into prints and solids. Then I organized them according to color. By placing the box on end, I have a grid of storage compartments in which I can stack my pieces of fabric.

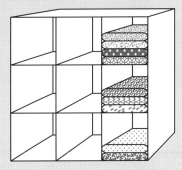

This way, I can see the end of each piece of fabric at a glance or easily remove just one section to look through it. This system solved the problem of always wanting the fabric at the bottom of the box. Another lucky break was that the box lids had been cut on three sides only, leaving a lovely, hinged cover. I can place the boxes on a shelf or stack them with the fabric facing me and the cover hinge at the top, making a convenient, covered storage system. It must have been karma, because the shelves in my new sewing room were just the right height for the boxes.

FLYING-GEESE-THE-FAST-WAY

With this technique, you will piece four Flying Geese segments at once, using two squares of fabric. Both of the squares are cut on the straight grain of the fabric and the segment will finish with all four sides on the straight grain. For the sake of ease, the directions are given for a Flying Geese segment with a finished measurement of 2" x 4". A table of different segment sizes appears on page 11. From two squares of fabric, you will get four Flying Geese segments, each 2½" x 4½". There will be a ¼"-wide seam allowance at the top of the goose triangle and at the tips of the goose triangle on the edge of the segment so that it finishes correctly to 2" x 4".

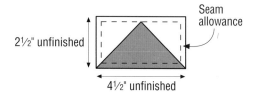

Making the Units

For 2" x 4" finished Flying Geese segments:

1. Cut 1 square, 5½" x 5½", from geese fabric. Cut 1 square, 6½" x 6½", from sky fabric.

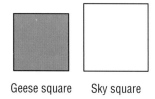

Geese square   Sky square

2. Carefully center the geese square on top of the sky square, right sides together, so that there is a ½"-wide seam allowance extending beyond the goose square on all edges.

Place a ruler diagonally across the squares and draw a line from corner to corner as shown above right. You can be sure the geese square is centered if the line you draw goes through all four corners exactly.

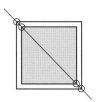

3. Sew exactly ¼" away from both sides of the diagonal line.

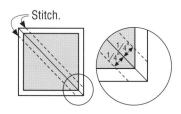

Stitch.

Measure the distance from the needle to the outside edge of the presser foot on your machine, making sure it is exactly ¼". If the measurement is ¼", use the edge of the foot as a seam guide. If the measurement is not exactly ¼", mark the stitching lines, using a sharp pencil and a ruler. On some sewing machines, the needle position can be moved so that the needle position is ¼" from the edge of the presser foot.

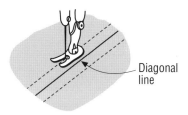

Diagonal line

4. Cut the square unit on the drawn center line to yield 2 pieces. Press seams toward the dark fabric. If you skip pressing, you will be sorry. (I am the voice of experience.)

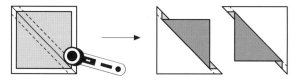

Cut on diagonal line.

5. Position the 2 squares, right sides together, matching the corners without seams. Make sure the sky fabric is on top of the geese fabric and vice versa. There will be excess fabric beyond the corners with the seam. Don't worry if these corners don't match exactly.

Note: Make sure the same fabric is not on top of itself, except along the center-seam area where the sky fabric overlaps. The diagonal seams should not match.

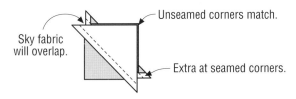

Unseamed corners match.
Sky fabric will overlap.
Extra at seamed corners.

6. Draw a diagonal from corner to corner across the seam.

New diagonal line

7. Repeat the sewing and cutting process in steps 3 and 4 to yield 2 pieces, each containing 2 Flying Geese segments. Press. The open area between the points of the geese will become the seam allowance at the top of each finished Flying Geese segment.

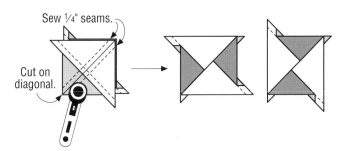

Sew ¼" seams.
Cut on diagonal.

Note: Seam allowances will show through the light fabric, but you can press to the dark fabric on both Flying Geese squares by flipping the seam allowance in the center where the sky fabric overlaps. Just slip your finger underneath the square and twist the seam to the darker fabric as you press.

Trimming the Segments

The next steps may seem a bit confusing at first. The biggest problem is getting comfortable with your square or ruler. The object of the process is to trim away the excess fabric to produce accurate Flying Geese units.

Remember that the finished unit is half as high as

it is wide. In this example, the finished Fying Geese unit is 2" high and 4" wide.

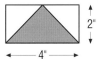

2"
4"

For a Flying Geese unit that finishes to 2" x 4", each unfinished unit must be trimmed to 2½" x 4½". This measurement includes the required ¼"-wide seam allowances.

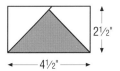

2½"
4½"

I have found it easiest to trim the Flying Geese units with a square ruler that has a marked diagonal line and graduated squares. My friend and directions guinea pig, Karen Walker, showed me this method. You can also use a quilter's ruler to trim them. Directions follow for each trimming method.

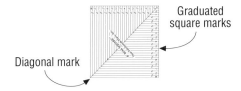

Graduated square marks
Diagonal mark

To trim with the Bias Square® ruler:
1. Look at the two pieced sections you just made. Lay them in front of you so one of the seams makes an uninterrupted diagonal across the square from the top right corner to the bottom left in each one. One of the pieces will have vertical geese and one will have horizontal geese.

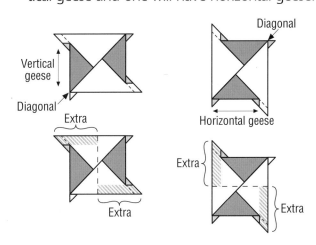

Diagonal
Vertical geese
Diagonal
Extra
Extra
Horizontal geese
Extra
Extra

2. Trim the section with the vertical geese triangles first. Align the top point of the geese triangle with the point where the 2¼" line meets the Bias Square's diagonal line. The ruler's diagonal line should run along the diagonal seam, aligning the 4½" line with the point where the two fabrics intersect. Trim along both edges of the ruler.

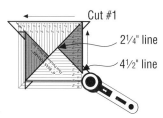

Cut #1
2¼" line
4½" line

The 2¼" measurement is very important! It is one-half of the unfinished width of the Flying Geese segment and ensures the top point of the geese triangle will be in the middle of the segment.

3. Flip the segment and trim the other sides in the same manner.

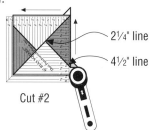

2¼" line
4½" line
Cut #2

4. Move the Bias Square down to trim the left-hand geese segment as shown. Position the 2½" line along the bottom edge of the vertical geese triangle, and the 2¼" mark through the top point of the geese triangle to frame a geese segment with the unfinished dimensions of 2½" x 4½". Cut along the ruler edges.

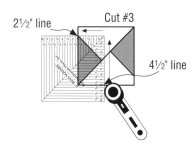

2½" line
Cut #3
4½" line

5. Turn and trim the remaining geese segment in the same manner as step 4. See illustration above right.

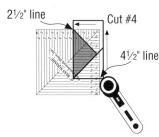

2½" line
Cut #4
4½" line

6. Align the top point of the upper geese triangle with the point where the 2¼" line meets the Bias Square's diagonal line. Make sure the ruler's diagonal line is on the diagonal seam, aligning the 4½" line at the point where the two fabrics intersect. Trim along the ruler edges.

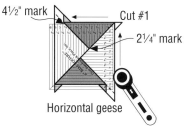

4½" mark
Cut #1
2¼" mark
Horizontal geese

7. Turn and trim the remaining two sides.

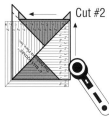

Cut #2

8. Move the Bias Square down to the lower geese triangle. Position the 2½" line along the bottom edge and the 2¼" line through the top point of the geese triangle. Cut along the Bias Square edges for an unfinished segment of 2½" x 4½".

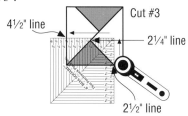

Cut #3
4½" line
2¼" line
2½" line

9. Trim the remaining segment as shown in step 8.

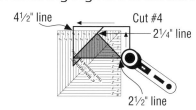

4½" line
Cut #4
2¼" line
2½" line

To trim with a quilter's ruler:

Using a 3"-wide ruler to trim the Flying Geese segments is much the same as using the Bias Square. If your ruler has a 45° diagonal line, trim the segment as shown in steps 2–8, above. If your ruler does not have a marked diagonal line:

1. Position the ruler with the 2¼" marking running through the top point of the geese triangle and the 2½" line running along the bottom of the geese triangle. The 4½" line should be where the fabrics intersect.

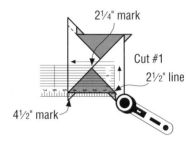

Cut along both edges of the ruler.

2. Turn the segment so the top point now points down. Position the ruler with the 2½" line along the bottom of the segment. The top point of the goose triangle should be at the 2¼" mark and the 4½" mark should be where the two fabrics intersect.

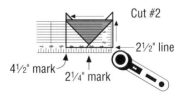

3. Repeat the trimming process with the remaining segments. If all has gone well, each of your geese segments should have a ¼"-wide seam allowance beyond the tip of the geese points. The side points

extend to the edges of the segment.

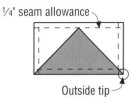

Note: The fastest way to add this technique to your personal bag of tricks is to practice, practice, practice! With that in mind, select a project from the next chapter, or create your own flight of fancy.

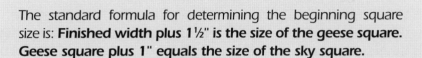
Square Size Table for Geese Segments

The standard formula for determining the beginning square size is: **Finished width plus 1½" is the size of the geese square. Geese square plus 1" equals the size of the sky square.**

Segment Width	Geese Square	Sky Square
2"	3½"	4½"
2½"	4"	5"
3"	4½"	5½"
3½"	5"	6"
4"	5½"	6½"
4½"	6"	7"
5"	6½"	7½"
5½"	7"	8"
6"	7½"	8½"

Counting the number of squares needed makes it easier to determine fabric requirements.

1. Count the number of Flying Geese segments needed.
2. Divide by 4, giving you the number of squares to cut from geese and sky fabric.

Number of Squares per Yard of 44"-wide Fabric

Size of Square	Squares per Yard	Size of Square	Squares per Yard
2"	357	5½"	42
2½"	208	6–6½"	30
3"	154	7"	25
3½"	108	7½"–8"	20
4"	80	8½"	16
4½"	63	9"–10½"	12
5"	56	11"	9

Flights of Fancy

Now that you've tried the piecing technique for fast geese, it is time to cut lots of squares and repeat, repeat, repeat the process. This is the best way to perfect this technique and become comfortable with it.

This chapter includes two specific learning projects. The first project is a wall hanging that uses the traditional Flying Geese straight-row set. It has a quick-pieced outer border that is made by switching the value placement in the Flying Geese segments. The second project is also a wall hanging combining Flying Geese and plain squares. Choose one of these projects or study the photos on pages 49–64 as inspiration for your own flight of fancy.

If you like to incorporate patchwork into garments, see pages 18–19 for information on how to use Flying Geese in your next piece of wearable art.

The Flying Geese block is equally effective in traditional and contemporary projects. Whether you make one for the bed or the wall, the important thing is to practice the technique. Please consider your first project as practice and refrain from cutting the pride of your fabric collection. A finished practice piece may not be your true desire but can always find a loving home as a Christmas or birthday gift or just as an expression of friendship—not to mention guild bazaars and white elephant exchanges! My practice pieces also find homes on the backs of chairs or on tabletops. Don't be afraid to make something for no other purpose than practice. This technique lends itself very nicely to small projects. All you need are the right-sized squares.

A flannel board or a design wall makes designing your own flight of fancy fun and easy. All of the projects in this book were designed on my padded wall. It was with true joy that I stapled fleece to a wall in my sewing room. I know from experience that this is not an option for everyone. However, if you have an easily accessible wall near your sewing area, consider mounting some café curtain rod brackets near the ceiling where they are not too noticeable. Hang a piece of fleece from a curtain rod while you work. You can design on the wall and put it away when you are not working.

Piece some Flying Geese and position them on the wall. Play with them until you find a pleasing arrangement, then sew them together quickly before they fly away.

TRADITIONAL FLYING GEESE

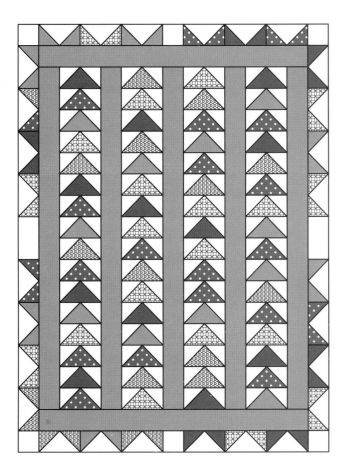

Finished Size: 32" x 40"
Color photo: page 64

Note: If you cut pieces for this quilt the traditional way, using templates, you would cut 276 triangles. With this method, you cut only 48 squares.

MATERIALS: 44"-wide fabric
1 yd. muslin or 1 yd. total of assorted light fabrics for sky
¼ yd. each of 4 rust, 8 green, and 4 brown prints for geese
¾ yd. for sashing
1¼ yds. for backing
½ yd. for binding
38" x 46" piece of batting

CUTTING

All measurements include ¼"-wide seam allowances.

From the muslin or light sky fabric, cut:
16 squares, each 6½" x 6½", for the center sky segments
8 squares, each 5½" x 5½", for the border geese segments
6 squares, each 2½" x 2½", for the border
2 rectangles, each 2½" x 4½", for the border

From the rust, green, and brown prints, cut:
16 squares, each 5½" x 5½". You will need 8 green, 4 rust, and 4 brown for the center geese segments.
8 squares, each 6½" x 6½". You will need 4 green and 4 brown for the border sky segments.

From the sashing fabric, cut:
5 strips, each 2½" x 32½"
2 strips, each 2½" x 26½"

DIRECTIONS

Note: I find that constructing the geese in groups of four helps to break up the work.

Flying Geese Segments

1. Using the 5½" and 6½" squares for the center geese segments, make Flying Geese. Follow the directions for "Flying-Geese-the-Fast-Way," beginning on page 8. Unfinished segments are 2½" x 4½".

2. Make 4 rows of 16 Flying Geese segments each. Arrange the geese segments to your liking on the design wall or flannel board. Begin by placing 1 segment of each print in each row.

Make 4.

3. Sew the 2½" x 32½" vertical sashing strips to the rows of geese, beginning and ending with the sashing strips as shown.

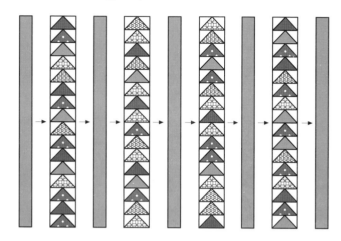

4. Sew the 2½" x 26½" horizontal sashing strips to the top and bottom of the center unit.

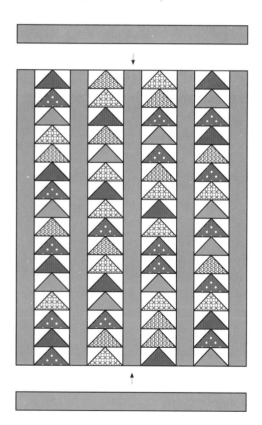

Border

1. For the side borders, sew 4 geese segments together, alternating brown and green prints.

Make 4.

2. Sew a light rectangle to a border row.

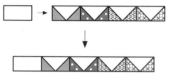

Make 2.

3. Joih a geese row to the other side of the rectangle as shown.

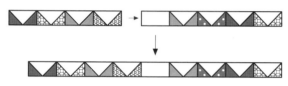

Make 2.

4. Sew completed border units to the sides of the center section.

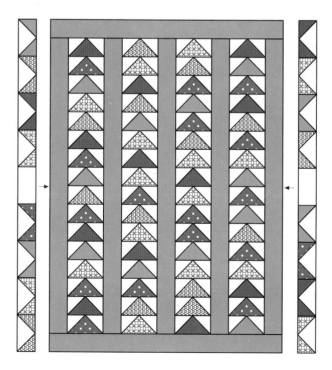

5. For the top and bottom borders, sew 3 Flying Geese segments together, alternating brown and green prints. Refer to the photo on page 64 for color placement at the corners.

 Make 2.

Make 2.

6. Add a light square to each end of 2 of the geese rows.

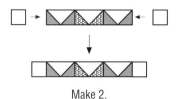

Make 2.

Add a light square to one end of the 2 remaining geese rows.

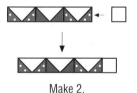

Make 2.

7. Join the rows to complete the top and bottom border units.

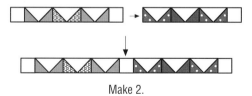

Make 2.

8. Sew the completed border units to the top and bottom of the center section to complete the practice quilt top.

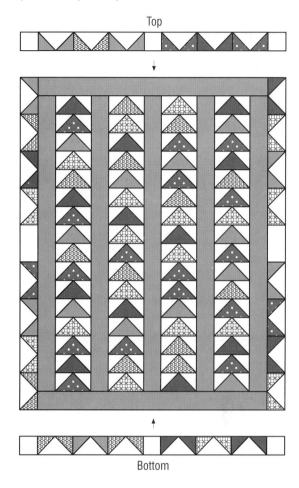

Top

Bottom

Note: The light squares and rectangles in the border are a simple setting solution. Setting the rows of geese together in the center section requires an uneven number of sashing strips. This adds an extra half-geese segment to the width. The side borders could be all geese (the light rectangle is the same size as a geese segment); however, that makes the light squares at the top and bottom more obvious. Eliminating the center geese segment on the side borders and replacing them with solid rectangles provides a simple, but wonderful, border solution.

9. See pages 77–79 for directions on finishing your quilt.

Geese and Squares

Finished Size: 36" x 36"
Color photo: page 50

Note: If you cut pieces for this quilt the traditional way, using templates, you would cut 264 triangles. With this method, you cut only 48 squares.

This quilt top is very simple to construct. It consists of squares made from two Flying Geese segments and solid squares the same size, plus a few rectangles on the outside edge. The finished size of the Flying Geese segments is 2" x 4", and the solid squares are 4" x 4".

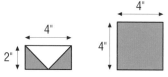

MATERIALS: 44"-wide fabric
½ yd. of muslin
½ yd. of dark blue print
1 yd. of blue solid
1 yd. of peach for solid squares
1¼ yds. for backing
½ yd. for binding
40" x 40" piece of batting

CUTTING

All measurements include ¼"-wide seam allowances.

From the muslin, cut:
14 squares, each 5½" x 5½", 12 for geese segments and 2 for border

From the dark blue print, cut:
6 squares, each 6½" x 6½", for sky
1 square, 5½" x 5½", for border

From the blue solid, cut:
9 squares, each 6½" x 6½", 6 for sky and 3 for border
4 squares, each 5½" x 5½", for border
4 squares, each 4½" x 4½", for border
16 rectangles, each 2½" x 4½", for border

From the peach, cut:
25 squares, each 4½" x 4½", for center unit
7 squares, each 6½" x 6½", for border
3 squares, each 5½" x 5½", for border

DIRECTIONS

Blocks

1. Using 12 muslin squares, each 5½" x 5½", and 6 dark blue print and 6 blue solid squares, each 6½" x 6½", make 48 Flying Geese segments. Follow the directions for "Flying-Geese-the-Fast-Way," beginning on page 8. These squares will yield 24 geese segments with dark blue print skies and 24 segments with blue solid skies. Unfinished segments are 2½" x 4½". Sew the segments together in pairs as shown to make a total of 24 squares. Press.

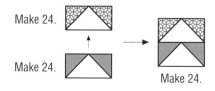

Make 24.

Make 24.

Make 24.

2. Arrange the Flying Geese squares in 7 rows. Alternate the squares with the 25 peach squares, each 4½" x 4½", as shown in the diagram on the next page. Note the direction of geese squares in each row.

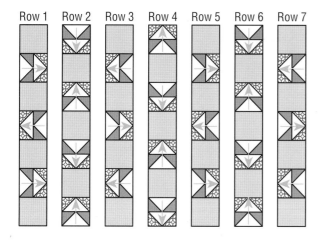

Row 1 Row 2 Row 3 Row 4 Row 5 Row 6 Row 7

Border

1. Using 2 blue solid and 2 peach squares, each 6½" x 6½", and 2 peach and 2 muslin squares, each 5½" x 5½", make Flying Geese. You will need 8 segments of each color combination.

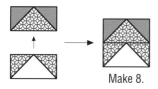

Make 8.   Make 8.

2. Sew geese segments in pairs to make 8 squares.

Make 8.

3. Using 1 blue solid and 1 peach square, each 6½" x 6½", and 1 peach and 1 dark blue print square, each 5½" x 5½", make Flying Geese, following directions for "Flying-Geese-the-Fast-Way," beginning on page 8.

Make 4.   Make 4.

4. Sew segments together in pairs to make 4 squares.

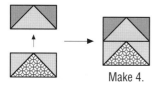

Make 4.

5. Using 4 peach squares, each 6½" x 6½", and 4 blue solid squares, each 5½" x 5½", make Flying Geese. You will need 16 geese segments.

Make 16.

6. Sew a geese segment to a plain rectangle to yield 16 squares.

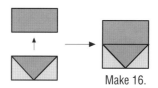

Make 16.

7. Using the assorted pieced squares and the 4 blue solid squares, arrange the borders as shown. Stitch.

Top and Bottom Border Strips
Make 2.

Side Border Strips
Make 2.

8. Sew completed border sections to each side as shown, then to the top and bottom to complete the quilt top.

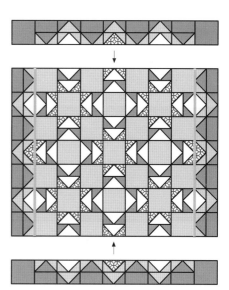

FLIGHTS-OF-FANCY GARMENTS

Color photo: page 62.

Flying Geese make wonderful garment embellishments. Patterns specifically made for pieced garments can be used, as well as regular commercial patterns. If you are looking for a pattern to use, there are a few points to keep in mind.

1. Choose a pattern without a lot of detail, such as extra seams, darts, or inset pockets.
2. Plan the piecing around buttonholes or zippers.
3. If you are adding batting, you may need to use a larger size pattern than you normally would to accommodate the added bulk.

Most woven fabrics can be successfully pieced. My jacket pictured on page 62 is made from 100% wool. I found wool easy to work with and very forgiving when it came time to match points. Once you have chosen the fabric and pattern, there are three ways to add pieced sections: flip and sew, whole piecing, and insertion.

Flip and Sew

1. Cut a foundation of fabric or fleece from the pattern piece. Cut it slightly larger than the actual pattern piece all around. Select a light color for the foundation fabric so that it will not show through your patchwork.
2. Position the pieced section on top of the foundation piece.

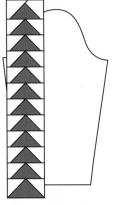

Sleeve pattern piece
Cut 1 of foundation fabric.

3. With right sides together, place the next fabric to be added on top of the pieced section as shown. Sew through all three layers, using a ¼"-wide seam.

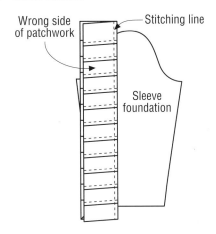

4. Open out the fabric piece and press. Trim excess, if necessary.

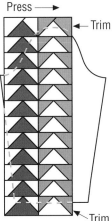

Place the next piece, right sides together, on top of the last piece sewn, matching raw edges and seam lines between the geese units. Stitch and press open. Continue adding pieces, sewing, flipping, and pressing until you have covered the foundation fabric.

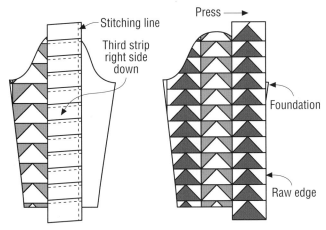

5. Lay the pattern on the covered foundation and trim to size.

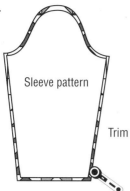

Whole Piecing

1. Sew a section of patchwork larger than necessary to fit the pattern piece.
2. Position the pattern piece on the patchwork and cut as shown. Repeat for the remaining pattern pieces, making sure to reverse patterns for left and right sides.

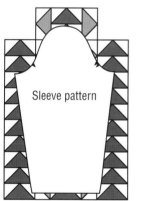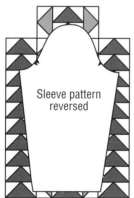

Cut a right and left sleeve.

If the garment is unlined, protect the patchwork by serging the seams, or underline the patchwork. Treat the patchwork and underlining as one piece when constructing the garment.

Insertion

1. If you want to insert a small section of patchwork into a larger garment piece, cut the finished size of the insertion out of the pattern piece. Add 1/4"-wide seam allowances to the cut edges of the pattern piece.

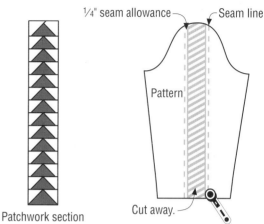

Patchwork section

2. Cut the garment sections from the desired fabric.
3. Stitch the patchwork section to the garment section with right sides together. Press seams toward the sleeve.

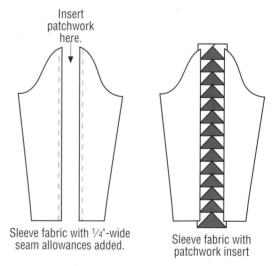

Sleeve fabric with 1/4"-wide seam allowances added.

Sleeve fabric with patchwork insert

Adding patchwork to garments is not difficult. Use your sense of adventure and don't be afraid to try it. These hints that I have learned from experience should help you avoid some problems! Just make sure you "think out" each piece carefully before you begin.

Note: Sections can be pieced and quilted and then added to a garment as above, especially if only the patchwork section has batting.

All the Blocks Are Geese Sampler

This sampler was designed to show how to apply the Flying Geese technique to standard quilt blocks. None of the blocks is difficult to piece, although some are more intricate than others. All of the blocks require easy, straight-seam sewing. If you are a beginner or experienced at machine quick-piecing, you will soon discover that this technique, when applied to standard blocks, has several advantages over existing piecing methods.

The Flying Geese segments are designed on a grid of squares, making it easy to determine the fabric square size needed for piecing the geese. If you want to make your quilt larger than 56" x 70", refer to the "Block Glossary" on pages 71–76 or consult your quilting library for more block possibilities. Also, you can repeat some of your favorite blocks from the twelve given here.

MATERIALS: 44"-wide fabric
For 12 blocks:
½ yd. each of 6 assorted colors
1¼ yds. muslin*
2¼ yds. for border and sashing
1 yd. for Flying Geese border segments

*Amount will vary depending on how you use it.

Note: To make geese segments for all blocks, refer to "Flying-Geese-the-Fast-Way," beginning on page 8.

Finished Quilt Size: 56" x 70"
Finished Block Size: 12" x 12"
Color photo: page 54

DUTCHMAN'S PUZZLE

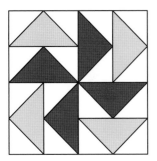

Finished Block Size:
12" x 12"
Finished Flying Geese
Segment: 3" x 6"

CUTTING

All measurements include ¼"-wide seam allowances.

From Fabric A for geese, cut:

1 square, 7½" x 7½"

From Fabric B for geese, cut:

1 square, 7½" x 7½"

From Fabric C for sky, cut:

2 squares, each 8½" x 8½"

DIRECTIONS

1. Using the 7½" and 8½" squares, make the Flying Geese segments. Trim the segments to the unfinished dimensions, 3½" x 6½", to yield 4 Flying Geese Segments A and 4 Segments B.

Segment A
Make 4.

Segment B
Make 4.

2. Sew Segment A to the top of Segment B. Make 4.
3. Lay out the Flying Geese sections as shown below. Join sections to complete the block.

Make 4.

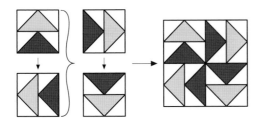

SEESAW

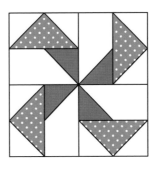

Finished Block Size:
12" x 12"
Finished Flying Geese
Segment: 3" x 6"

CUTTING

All measurements include ¼"-wide seam allowances.

From Fabric A for geese, cut:

1 square, 7½" x 7½"

From Fabric C for sky, cut:

1 square, 8½" x 8½"
2 rectangles, each 3½" x 10"

From Fabric B, cut:

2 squares, each 4½" x 4½"

DIRECTIONS

1. Using the 7½" and 8½" squares, make 4 Flying Geese segments. Trim to 3½" x 6½" to yield 4 Flying Geese segments.

Make 4.

2. Mark the center of each 3½" x 10" rectangle by folding it in half crosswise with right sides together. Press lightly. Mark the center of each 4½" square by folding it in half, wrong sides together. Press. Leave the squares folded and open the rectangles.

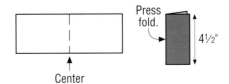

Press fold.

4½"

Center

3. Position a folded square on the right side of a rectangle, matching pressed center lines. Unfold the square. The square should extend exactly ½" above and below the rectangle as shown.

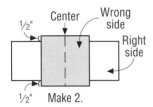

Make 2.

4. Mark a diagonal line across the 4½" square from the top left to the bottom right corner.

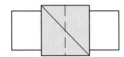

5. Sew along both sides, ¼" away from the drawn diagonal line.

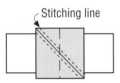

Stitching line

6. Cut the rectangles on the drawn diagonal line. Press seams toward the darker fabric.

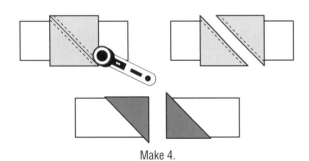

Make 4.

7. Place your ruler or square on the rectangle with the right edge of the ruler on the intersection of the fabrics at the 3½" mark, and the left edge of the rectangle on the 6½" mark. Trim the rectangles to 3½" x 6½".

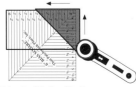

Trim to 3½" x 6½".

8. Sew a Flying Geese segment to the top edge of each rectangle segment. Make 4.

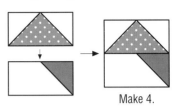

Make 4.

9. Lay out the Flying Geese/rectangle sections as shown. Join the segments to complete the block.

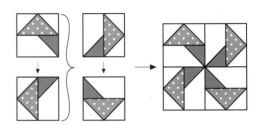

NEXT-DOOR NEIGHBOR

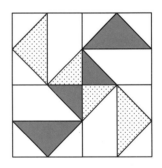

Finished Block Size:
12" x 12"
Finished Flying Geese
Segment: 3" x 6"

CUTTING

All measurements include ¼"-wide seam allowances.

From Fabric A for geese, cut:
1 square, 7½" x 7½"
1 square, 4½" x 4½"

From Fabric B for geese, cut:
1 square, 7½" x 7½"
1 square, 4½" x 4½"

From Fabric C for sky, cut:
2 squares, each 8½" x 8½"
2 rectangles, each 3½" x 10"

DIRECTIONS

1. Using the 7½" and 8½" squares, make 4 Flying Geese segments. Trim to 3½" x 6½" to yield 4 segments with Fabric A geese, and 4 with Fabric B geese.

Fabric A Geese
Make 2.

Fabric B Geese
Make 2.

2. Mark the center of each 3½" x 10" rectangle by folding it in half crosswise, right sides together. Press lightly. Mark the center of each 4½" square by folding it in half, wrong sides together. Press.

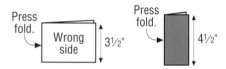

Leave the squares folded and open the rectangles.

3. Position a folded square on the right side of a rectangle, matching pressed middle lines. Open the square. The square should extend exactly ½" above and ½" below the rectangle as shown.

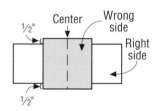

4. Mark a diagonal line across the 4½" square, from top left to bottom right corner.

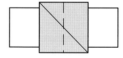

5. Sew along both sides, ¼" away from the drawn diagonal line.

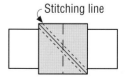

6. Cut the rectangle on the drawn diagonal line. Press seams toward the darker fabric.

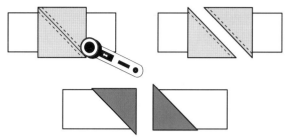

Make 2 of each color.

7. Place your ruler or square on the rectangle with the right edge of the ruler on the intersection of the fabrics at the 3½" mark, and the left edge of the rectangle on the 6½" mark. Trim the rectangles to 3½" x 6½".

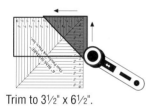

Trim to 3½" x 6½".

8. Pair a Flying Geese segment with a matching rectangle as shown. Make 4. Set aside remaining geese for another project.

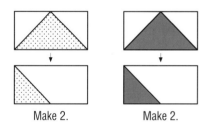

Make 2.   Make 2.

9. Lay out the Flying Geese/rectangle sections in the order shown below. Join sections to complete the block.

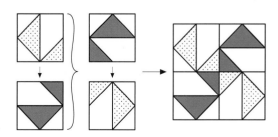

KING'S CROWN

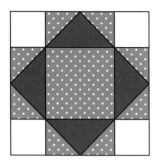

Finished Block Size:
   12" x 12"
Finished Flying Geese
   Segment: 3" x 6"

CUTTING

All measurements include ¼"-wide seam allowances.

From Fabric A for sky, cut:

 1 square, 8½" x 8½"
   1 square, 6½" x 6½", for center

From Fabric B for geese, cut:

 1 square, 7½" x 7½"

From Fabric C for corners, cut:

 4 squares, each 3½" x 3½"

DIRECTIONS

1. Using the 7½" and 8½" squares, make 4 Flying Geese segments. Trim to 3½" x 6½" to yield 4 segments.

Make 4.

2. Sew a Flying Geese segment between two 3½" x 3½" squares. Make 2 rows.

Make 2.

3. Sew the center square between 2 Flying Geese segments as shown. Make 1 row.

Make 1.

4. Join the rows to complete the block.

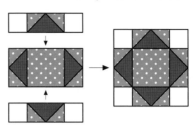

WILD GOOSE CHASE (VARIATION)

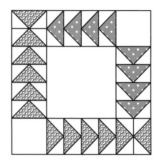

Finished Block Size:
   12" x 12"
Finished Flying Geese
   Segment: 1½" x 3"

CUTTING

All measurements include ¼"-wide seam allowances.

From Fabric A for geese, cut:

 2 squares, each 4½" x 4½"

From Fabric B for geese, cut:

 3 squares, each 4½" x 4½"

From Fabric C for sky, cut:

5 squares, each 5½" x 5½"
2 squares, each 3½" x 3½", for corners
1 square, 6½" x 6½", for center

DIRECTIONS

1. Using the 4½" and 5½" squares, make Flying Geese segments. Trim to 2" x 3½", to yield a total of 20 segments. You will need 8 with Fabric A geese and 12 with Fabric B geese.

Fabric A Geese   Fabric B Geese
Make 8.   Make 12.

2. Assemble the following rows to make 6 sections:
4 segments of Fabric A geese. Make 2.
4 segments of Fabric B geese. Make 2.
2 segments of Fabric B geese. Make 2.

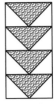

Make 2.

Make 2.   Make 2.

3. Lay out the Flying Geese sections and the plain squares in the order shown below. Join the sections to complete the block.

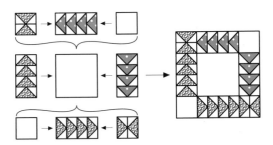

Aunt Sukey's Choice

Finished Block Size:
  12" x 12"
Finished Flying Geese
  Segment: 2" x 4"

CUTTING
All measurements include ¼"-wide seam allowances.

From Fabric A for geese, cut:
 1 square, 5½" x 5½"
1 square, 4½" x 4½", for center

From Fabric B for sky, cut:
 1 square, 6½" x 6½"

From Fabric C for geese and sky, cut:
 1 square, 6½" x 6½"
1 square, 5½" x 5½"
1 square, 5" x 5"
2 rectangles, each 4½" x 5"

From Fabric D, cut:
 1 square, 5" x 5"

DIRECTIONS

1. Using the 5½" and 6½" squares, make Flying Geese segments. Trim to 2½" x 4½" to yield 8 segments. You will need 4 with light skies and 4 with dark skies.

Make 4.   Make 4.

2. Pair a Fabric A, light-sky goose segment with a Fabric B, dark-sky goose segment as shown. Make 4.

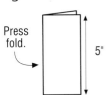

Make 4.

3. To assemble the corner sections, mark the center of two 5" squares by folding them in half and lightly pressing the fold.

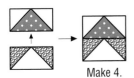

Press fold.

5"

Open the squares and stack right sides together, matching center folds. Sew along both sides of the center fold, ¼" away from it.

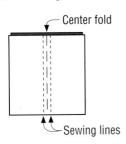

Center fold

Sewing lines

Cut on the fold line, open the squares, and press the seams toward the darker fabric.

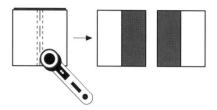

4. Center a square unit on top of a 4½" x 5" rectangle, right sides together, as shown. Draw a vertical line at the 2½" center point.

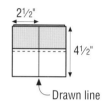

Sew ¼" away from the drawn line, along both sides as shown.

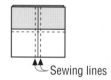

Cut apart along the drawn line. Open and press.

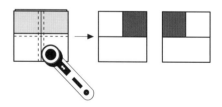

5. Arrange the Flying Geese/center square/corner sections as shown. Join the sections to complete the block.

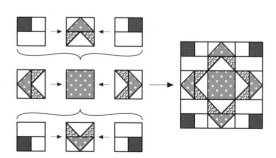

THE CYPRESS

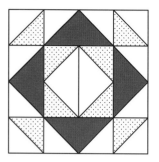

Finished Block Size:
 12" x 12"
Finished Flying Geese
 Segment: 3" x 6"

CUTTING

All measurements include ¼"-wide seam allowances.

Note: If you choose the same color combinations as those used in the Next-Door Neighbor block on pages 22–23, you can use the Flying Geese segments left over from that block for the center section in this one.

From Fabric A for sky, cut:
1 square, 8½" x 8½"
2 squares, each 3⅞" x 3⅞", for corners

From Fabric B for geese, cut:
1 square, 7½" x 7½"

From Fabric C for geese and sky, cut:
1 square, 8½" x 8½"
1 square, 7½" x 7½"
2 squares, each 3⅞" x 3⅞", for corners

DIRECTIONS

1. Using the 7½" and 8½" squares, make Flying Geese segments. Trim to 3½" x 6½" to yield 8 segments. You will need segments with both light and dark skies.

Make 4.   Make 2.

2. Sew 2 segments with Fabric C geese together for the center section. Set remaining segments aside.

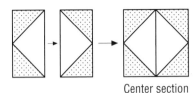

Center section

3. To assemble the corner sections, pair a 3⅞" square of Fabric A with a 3⅞" square of Fabric C. Mark a diagonal line from the top left corner to the bottom right corner on each pair as shown.

Drawn line

Make 2.

4. Sew ¼" away from the drawn line, along both sides as shown.

Stitching lines

Cut squares on the drawn diagonal line. Open and press seam toward the darker fabric.

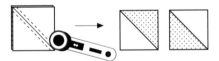

5. Arrange the sections in order as shown. Join sections to complete the block.

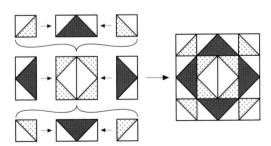

CAPITAL T

Finished Block Size:
12" x 12"
Finished Flying Geese
Segment: 2" x 4"

CUTTING
All measurements include ¼"-wide seam allowances.

From Fabric A for sky, cut:
2 squares, each 6½" x 6½"
2 squares, each 4⅞" x 4⅞"

From Fabric B for geese, cut:
2 squares, each 5½" x 5½"
2 squares, each 4⅞" x 4⅞"
1 square, 4½" x 4½", for center

DIRECTIONS
1. Using the 5½" and 6½" squares, make Flying Geese segments. Trim to 2½" x 4½" to yield 8 segments.

Make 8.

2. Sew 2 Flying Geese segments together as shown. Make 4.

Make 4.

3. To assemble the corner sections, pair the 4⅞" x 4⅞" squares, 1 of Fabric A with 1 of Fabric B. Stack the squares right sides together. Draw a diagonal line, from the top left corner to the bottom right corner, on each stack of squares.

Drawn line

4. Sew ¼" away from the drawn line, along both sides as shown.

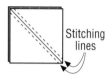

Stitching lines

5. Cut the squares on the drawn diagonal line. Open and press the seam toward the darker fabric.

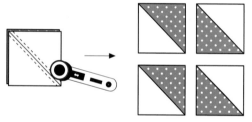

Make 4.

6. Arrange the Flying Geese sections/corner squares as shown below. Join sections to complete the block.

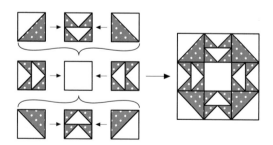

EVENING STAR

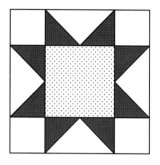

Finished Block Size:
   12" x 12"
Finished Flying Geese
   Segment: 3" x 6"

CUTTING

All measurements include ¼"-wide seam allowances.

From Fabric A for center, cut:
 1 square, 6½" x 6½"

From Fabric B for sky, cut:
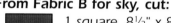 1 square, 8½" x 8½"

From Fabric C for geese, cut:
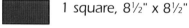 1 square, 7½" x 7½"
4 squares, each 3½" x 3½", for corners

DIRECTIONS

1. Using the 7½" and 8½" squares, make Flying Geese segments. Trim to 3½" x 6½", to yield 4 segments.

Make 4.

2. Assemble the sections as shown below and join to complete the block.

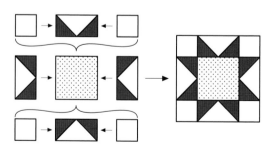

STARS AND SQUARES

Finished Block Size:
  12" x 12"
Finished Flying Geese
  Segment: Large - 3" x 6"
    Small - 1½" x 3"

CUTTING

All measurements include ¼"-wide seam allowances.

From Fabric A for sky (large Flying Geese), cut:
 1 square, 8½" x 8½"

From Fabric B for sky (small Flying Geese), cut:
 1 square, 5½" x 5½"

From Fabric C for geese, cut:
 1 square, 4½" x 4½"
4 squares, each 2" x 2"
4 squares, each 3½" x 3½"
1 square, 7½" x 7½"

From Fabric D for center, cut:
 1 square, 3½" x 3½"

DIRECTIONS

1. Using the 4½" and 5½" squares for the small Flying Geese segments, and the 7½" and 8½" squares for the large geese segments, make the Flying Geese. Trim the small segments to 2" x 3½", and the large segments to 3½" x 6½".

Small Flying Geese   Large Flying Geese
    Make 4.   Make 4.

You will need 4 small segments and 4 large segments.

2. Assemble the small Flying Geese segments, small squares, and the center square into 3 rows as shown.

3. Join sections to complete the center.

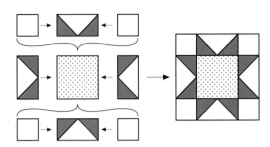

4. Assemble the large Flying Geese segments and the completed center "star" into 3 rows as shown. Join sections to complete the block.

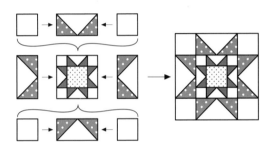

FREE TRADE

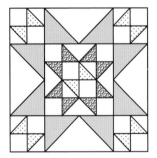

Finished Block Size:
  12" x 12"
Finished Flying Geese
  Segment: Large - 3" x 6"
    Small - 1½" x 3"

CUTTING

All measurements include ¼"-wide seam allowances.

From Fabric A for half-square triangle units, cut:
 5 squares, each 2⅜" x 2⅜"

From Fabric B for sky (small geese), cut:
 1 square, 5½" x 5½"

From Fabric C for geese, cut:

1 square, 4½" x 4½", for small geese
14 squares, each 2" x 2", for corners
5 squares, each 2⅜" x 2⅜", for half-
  square triangle units
1 square, 7½" x 7½", for large geese

From Fabric D for sky, cut:

1 square, 8½" x 8½"

DIRECTIONS

1. Using the 4½" and 5½" squares for the small geese segments, and the 7½" and 8½" squares for the large geese segments, make the Flying Geese. Trim the small segments to 2" x 3½", and the large segments to 3½" x 6½".

Small Flying Geese   Large Flying Geese
Make 4.   Make 4.

You will need 4 small geese segments and 4 large geese segments.

2. To assemble the corner sections, pair a 2⅜" square of Fabric A with a square of Fabric C. Stack the squares right sides together. Draw a diagonal line, from the top left corner to the bottom right corner, on each stack of squares.

Drawn line

3. Sew ¼" away from the drawn line, along both sides as shown.

Stitching lines

4. Cut the squares on the drawn diagonal line. Open and press seam toward the darker fabric. You need 10 half-square triangle units for the block center and the corner four-patch units.

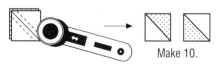

Make 10.

5. Assemble a four-patch unit, using two 2" squares and 2 half-square triangle units as shown.
6. Join the four-patch units. Make 5.

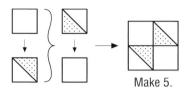

Make 5.

7. Assemble the small Flying Geese segments, a four-patch unit, and the plain squares into 3 rows as shown.
8. Join the rows to complete the center square.

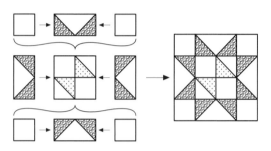

9. Arrange the large Flying Geese segments, the center square, and the corner four-patch units as shown. Join sections to complete the block.

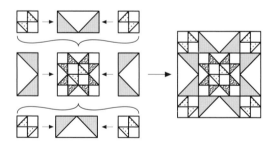

CROWN AND STAR

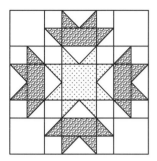

Finished Block Size:
 12" x 12"
Finished Flying Geese
 Segment: 1½" x 3"

CUTTING

All measurements include ¼"-wide seam allowances.

From Fabric A for sky and center, cut:
 1 square, 5½" x 5½"
 1 square, 3½" x 3½"

From Fabric B for sky, rectangles, and triangles, cut:
 1 square, 5½" x 5½"
 4 rectangles, each 2" x 3½"
 4 squares, each 2⅜" x 2⅜"

From Fabric C for geese, triangles, and corners, cut:
 2 squares, each 4½" x 4½"
 12 squares, each 2" x 2"
 4 squares, each 2⅜" x 2⅜"
 4 squares, each 3½" x 3½"

DIRECTIONS

1. Using the 4½" and 5½" squares, make Flying Geese segments. Trim to 2" x 3½" to yield 8 segments. You need 1 set of Flying Geese with Fabric A sky and 1 set with Fabric B sky.

2. Using the Fabric A sky, small squares, and center, assemble the block center.

Fabric A Sky   Fabric B Sky

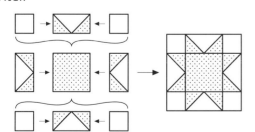

3. Sew a rectangle to a Fabric B sky segment for the crown section as shown. Make 4.

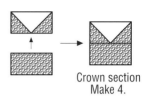
Crown section
Make 4.

4. To assemble the corner sections, pair a 2⅜" square of Fabric B with one of Fabric C. Stack the squares with right sides together.

5. Draw a diagonal line, from the top left corner to the bottom right corner, on each stack of squares.

Drawn line

6. Sew ¼" away from the drawn line, along both sides as shown.

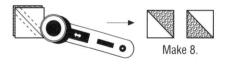
Stitching lines

7. Cut the squares on the drawn diagonal line. Open and press the seam toward the dark fabric. You need 8 half-square triangle units.

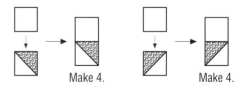
Make 8.

8. Sew a 2" x 2" square of Fabric C to each half-square triangle unit as shown.

Make 4.   Make 4.

9. Sew a square/half-square triangle unit to opposite sides of each crown section (step 3) as shown.

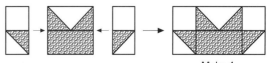
Make 4.

10. Assemble the crown sections, corner squares, and center "star" in 3 rows as shown. Join the rows to complete the block.

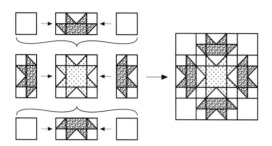

Quilt Assembly and Finishing

CUTTING

All measurements include ¼"-wide seam allowances.

Follow the cutting diagram to cut the sashing and border pieces.

Note: In the quilt pictured on page 54, the top and bottom borders required creative problem solving. The finished size of the Flying Geese segment caused the top and bottom pieced border strips to be 1" too long. To compensate, a slightly deeper than ¼"-wide seam allowance was taken when the Flying Geese segments were sewn together. In the following cutting directions, the width of the left and right side sashing strips has been increased by ½" each so the pieced border will fit without adjusting the seam allowances.

From the sashing/border fabric, cut:
8 strips, each 3½" x 12½"
2 squares, each 4⅜" x 4⅜", for half-square triangle units
8 squares, each 9½" x 9½", for skies
2 strips, each 4" x 57½", for side sashing
2 strips, each 3½" x 49½", for top and bottom sashing
3 strips, each 3½" x 42½", for horizontal sashing between block rows

From your choice of fabric for geese, cut:
8 squares, each 8½" x 8½"
2 squares, each 4⅜" x 4⅜", for half-square triangle units

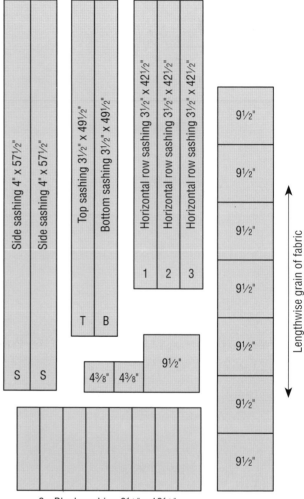

Side sashing 4" x 57½"
Side sashing 4" x 57½"
Top sashing 3½" x 49½"
Bottom sashing 3½" x 49½"
Horizontal row sashing 3½" x 42½"
Horizontal row sashing 3½" x 42½"
Horizontal row sashing 3½" x 42½"

1 2 3

T B

S S

4⅜" 4⅜"

9½"

9½"
9½"
9½"
9½"
9½"
9½"
9½"

Lengthwise grain of fabric

8 - Block sashing 3½" x 12½"

DIRECTIONS

Sashing

1. Arrange the sampler blocks in 4 rows of 3 blocks each. Sew a 3½" x 12½" sashing strip between the blocks as shown.

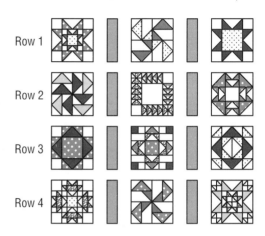

2. Sew a 3½" x 42½" sashing strip between each block row as shown.

3. Sew a 4" x 57½" strip to each side of the quilt top. Pin as shown and ease in any fullness. (See the note on top and bottom borders on page 32.)

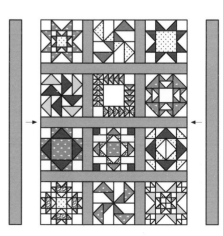

4. Add the top and bottom sashing strips to the quilt top. Pin as shown and ease in any fullness.

Border

1. Using the 8½" squares and the 9½" squares, make Flying Geese segments. Trim to 4" x 7½", to yield 32 segments.

2. Pair a 4⅜" square of sashing fabric with a 4⅜" square of your choice of fabric. Stack squares, right sides together. Make 2 stacks. Draw a diagonal line, from the top left corner to the bottom right corner, on each stack of squares.

Drawn line

3. Sew ¼" away from the drawn line, along both sides as shown.

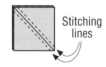

Stitching lines

4. Cut the squares on the drawn diagonal line. Open and press the seam toward the darker fabric. You need 4 half-square triangle units.

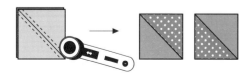

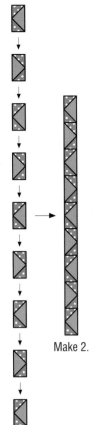

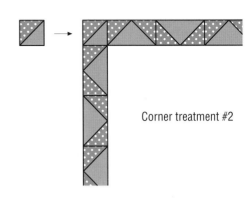

Corner treatment #2

5. Sew 9 Flying Geese segments together, alternating pieces with the point up and the point down as shown. Make 2 side borders.

Make 2.

8. Sew the top and bottom borders to the quilt, pinning as shown and easing in any fullness.

Make 2.

9. Finish your Flying Geese Sampler quilt, following the directions on pages 77–79.

6. Sew 7 Flying Geese segments together, alternating the point up and point down as shown. Make 2 for top and bottom borders.

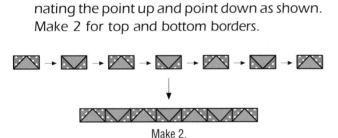

Make 2.

7. Select a corner treatment from those shown (see page 70) and sew a half-square triangle unit to each end of the remaining top and bottom border strips.

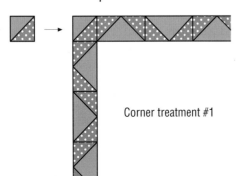

Corner treatment #1

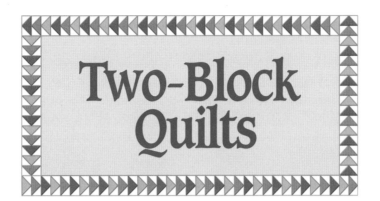

Two-Block Quilts

Wonderful new patterns often emerge when two different quilt blocks are set together. Neon Desert and Spring Mosaic each consist of simple, straight-pieced blocks.

The Evening Star and Album blocks make up the Spring Mosaic quilt. In addition to the Flying Geese, there are half-square triangle units for the corners of the inner border and rectangles for the outer border.

The Neon Desert quilt was named for its bright colors. It has Cup and Saucer and Neon Star blocks. Each block has corner sections of half-square triangle units and sections of two Flying Geese segments.

When choosing blocks for two-block quilts, there are a few things to consider. First, both blocks should be equally divided on a grid. Refer to the Block Glossary on pages 71–76 for information on grids. Both blocks for Spring Mosaic are on a 4 x 4 square grid. The blocks used in Neon Desert are on a 3 x 3 square grid.

4x4 square grid

Evening Star
on a 4x4 square grid

3x3 square grid   Cup and Saucer
on a 3x3 square grid

Second, block intersections should form new patterns. In the Neon Desert quilt, the corners, blocks, and center sections of the blocks match up to continue the pattern across the quilt.

Third, when designing your quilt, add a partial-block border to complete the patterns. This partial-block border is called a "goosed border."

Finally, to balance the top with the same block in all four corners, assemble an uneven number of blocks. For example, plan your quilt top with five rows of three blocks each (15).

Spring Mosaic

Evening Star block

Album block

Finished Quilt Size: 68" x 84"
Finished Block Size: 8" x 8"
Finished Flying Geese Segment:
    2" x 4" for center section
    4" x 8" for inner border
Color photo: page 49

MATERIALS: 44"-wide fabric

1 yd. each of dark purple, lavender, dark green, and green solid

1 yd. light print for center blocks

1¾ yds. medium green print for outside blocks

2 yds. muslin for inner border strips* and outer border blocks

6 yds. for backing

1 yd. for binding

72" x 88" piece of batting

*Cut from the length of fabric to eliminate a seamed inner border.

CUTTING

All measurements include ¼"-wide seam allowances.

For each Evening Star block, cut:

 1 square, 5½" x 5½", of light print for geese

4 squares, each 2½" x 2½", of light print for corners

 1 square, 6½" x 6½", of green solid for sky*

 1 square, 4½" x 4½", of dark green for center

*For Evening Star blocks, make 6 segments with green solid star points and 2 with dark green star points.

For each Album block, cut:

 1 square, 5½" x 5½", of lavender for geese

4 squares, each 2½" x 2½", of lavender for corners

 1 square, 6½" x 6½", of light print for skies

 1 square, 4½" x 4½", of purple for center

DIRECTIONS

Note: To make geese segments for all blocks and border units, refer to "Flying-Geese-the-Fast-Way," beginning on page 8.

Evening Star Block

1. Using the 5½" and 6½" squares, make Flying Geese segments. Trim to 2½" x 4½", to yield 4 segments.

2. Assemble the segments, corners, and center square as shown below, then join to complete the block. Make 8 Evening Star blocks.

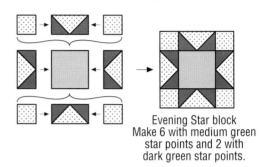

Evening Star block
Make 6 with medium green star points and 2 with dark green star points.

Album Block

1. Using the 5½" and 6½" squares, make Flying Geese segments. Trim to 2½" x 4½" to yield 4 segments.

2. Assemble the segments, corners, and center square as shown below. Join to complete the block. Make 7 Album blocks.

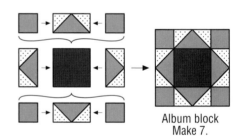

Album block
Make 7.

Center

1. Assemble 5 rows of 3 blocks each as shown.

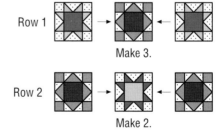

Row 1

Make 3.

Row 2

Make 2.

2. Join the rows to complete the center unit.

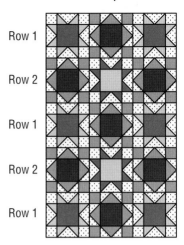

Row 1
Row 2
Row 1
Row 2
Row 1

Flying Geese Inner Border

Note: Reverse the color placement in the Flying Geese segments to finish the secondary pattern. Make 10 dark geese with light skies for the Evening Star blocks, and 6 light geese with dark skies (4 lavender and 2 purple) for the Album blocks.

CUTTING

All measurements include ¼"-wide seam allowances.

From the dark green, cut:
2 squares, each 5½" x 5½"

From the light print, cut:
2 squares, each 6½" x 6½"
2 squares, each 5½" x 5½"

From the lavender, cut:
1 square, 6½" x 6½"
20 squares, each 2½" x 2½"

From the purple, cut:
1 square, 6½" x 6½"

From the green solid, cut:
15 squares, each 2½" x 2½"

ASSEMBLY

1. Using the 5½" and 6½" squares, make Flying

Geese segments. Trim to 2½" x 4½", to yield 16 segments. For color placement, see the quilt photo on page 49. Save the extra 2 purple and 2 green segments for another project.

2. Position the Flying Geese segments and squares as shown; join the segments.

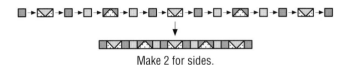

Make 2 for top and bottom.

Make 2 for sides.

3. Sew a border row to each side of the quilt top, then add the top and bottom rows as shown. This finishes the secondary patterns formed by the two blocks.

Middle Border

The pieced middle border consists of three sections, a 2"-wide plain inner strip, a strip of Flying Geese segments, and a 2"-wide plain outer strip. The Flying Geese segments are doubled in size to 4" x 8", giving the quilt a more spacious feel.

Note: The size of the Flying Geese segment can be doubled because the height of the Flying Geese inner border plus the width of the plain inner border strip adds 8" to the length and width of the quilt top. When adding a Flying Geese inner border and a plain border strip, make the combined width of these borders equal to the width of the Flying Geese segments used in the blocks. You can use either the same size Flying Geese that you used in the blocks or you can double the size.

CUTTING

All measurements include ¼"-wide seam allowances.

Follow the directions on page 67 for measuring the quilt top to determine the length of each border strip.

From the muslin, cut:
2 strips, each 2½" x 44½", for the inner side strips
2 strips, each 2½" x 32½", for the inner top and
    bottom strips
2 strips, each 2½" x 56½", for the outer side strips
2 strips, each 2½" x 44½", for the outer top and
    bottom strips
6 squares, each 10½" x 10½", for skies
2 squares, each 4⅞" x 4⅞", for corners

From the lavender, cut:
2 squares, each 9½" x 9½", for geese
1 square, 4⅞" x 4⅞", for corners

From the green solid, cut:
2 squares, each 9½" x 9½", for geese
1 square, 4⅞" x 4⅞", for corners

From the purple, cut:
1 square, 9½" x 9½", for geese

From the dark green, cut:
1 square, 9½" x 9½", for geese

ASSEMBLY

1. Sew a plain inner border strip to each side of the quilt top, then to the top and bottom edges.

2. Using the 9½" and 10½" squares, make Flying Geese segments. Trim to 4½" x 8½" to yield 24 segments. You need 8 lavender and 8 green solid geese, and 4 purple and 4 dark green geese.

3. With right sides together, pair a green solid square with a muslin square and a lavender square with a muslin square. Stack squares. Draw a diagonal line, from the top left corner to the bottom right corner, on each stack of squares.

Drawn line

4. Sew ¼" away from the drawn line, along both sides as shown.

Stitching lines

5. Cut the squares on the drawn diagonal line. Open and press the seam toward the darker fabric. You need 4 half-square triangle units, 2 each of green solid and lavender.

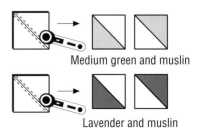

Medium green and muslin

Lavender and muslin

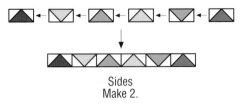

Sides
Make 2.

6. Using the quilt diagram as a guide, lay out the Flying Geese segments and squares; join the segments. Save the remaining 2 lavender and 2 green solid segments for another project.

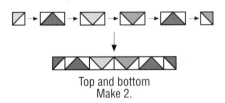

Top and bottom
Make 2.

7. Sew the side borders to the quilt top and then add the top and bottom borders.

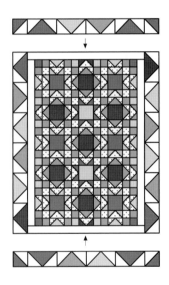

8. Sew a plain outer border strip to each side of the quilt top, then add the top and bottom borders.

Outer Border

The outer border consists of Evening Star and Album blocks set between strips made of Flying Geese segments and plain squares. Refer to the quilt photo on page 49 for color placement.

CUTTING

All measurements include ¼"-wide seam allowances.

For each Evening Star block, cut:
1 square, 5½" x 5½", of muslin for geese
1 square, 6½" x 6½", of green solid for sky*
1 square, 4½" x 4½", of dark green for center
4 squares, each 2½" x 2½", of muslin for corners

*For Evening Star blocks, make 8 with green solid star points, 4 with medium green print star points, and 2 with dark green star points.

For each Album block, cut:
1 square, 5½" x 5½", of lavender or purple for geese*
1 square, 6½" x 6½", of muslin for sky
1 square, 4½" x 4½", of purple for center
4 squares, each 2½" x 2½", of purple for corners

*Make 6 geese lavender and 8 geese purple.

For the setting Geese and Squares, cut:
9 squares, each 5½" x 5½", of medium green print
9 squares, each 6½" x 6½", of medium green print
56 rectangles, each 2½" x 4½", of medium green print
4 rectangles, each 2½" x 8½", of medium green print
4 rectangles, each 2½" x 6½", of medium green print
4 squares, each 2½" x 2½", of medium green print
9 squares, each 6½" x 6½", of muslin
9 squares, each 5½" x 5½", of muslin
16 squares, each 2½" x 2½", of muslin
16 squares, each 2½" x 2½", of purple

ASSEMBLY

1. Using the 5½" and 6½" squares, make Flying Geese segments. Trim to 2½" x 4½" to yield 4 segments.

2. Make 14 Evening Star blocks, following the directions on page 28.

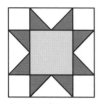

Evening Star Block
Make 14.

3. Using the 5½" and 6½" squares, make Flying Geese segments. Trim to 2½" x 4½" to yield 4 segments.

4. Make 14 Album blocks, following the directions on page 36.

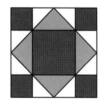

Album Block
Make 14.

5. For each side border, sew 3 Evening Star and 4 Album blocks together, beginning and ending each row with an Album block.

Side Border Segment
Make 2.

6. For each remaining border strip, sew 3 Album and 2 Evening Star blocks together, beginning and ending each with an Album block.

Top and Bottom Border Segment
Make 2.

Note: There are four Evening Star blocks remaining for the corners. Before you sew these blocks to the corners, add the following Flying Geese segments and squares to the top and bottom of each side border.

7. Using the remaining 5½" and 6½" squares, make Flying Geese segments. Trim to 2½" x 4½" to yield 8 segments. Two sets will have print geese, and 2 sets will have muslin geese.

Medium Print Geese   Muslin Geese
Make 8.   Make 8.

8. Add a muslin square to each side of the segment with muslin geese, and add purple squares to those with print geese for border units.

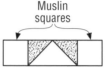 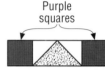

Muslin squares   Purple squares

Make 8 for border.   Make 8 for border.

9. Sew a completed unit to each end of the side pieced border strips.

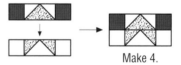

Make 2.

10. Using the remaining segments, make 4 units as shown.

Make 4.

11. Sew a completed unit to each end of the top and bottom border strips.

12. Sew an Evening Star block to each end of the top and bottom border strips.

13. Using the 5½" and 6½" squares, make Flying Geese segments. Trim to 2½" x 4½", to yield 56 segments. You need 28 segments with muslin geese, and 28 segments with medium green print geese.

Make 28.   Make 28.

14. Make 2 side border strips, using 7 geese segments and 8 rectangles in each. Be sure to alternate the direction of the geese as shown.

Make 4.

15. Assemble the top and bottom strips, using squares, remaining rectangles, and Flying Geese segments as shown.

Make 2.

16. Join the completed strips to the pieced side borders, then add to the sides of the quilt top.

17. Join the completed strips to the top and bottom border pieces, then add these units to the top and bottom of the quilt top.

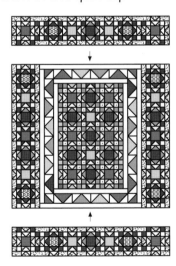

Whew! Lots of pieces, but worth it—and faster than it looks!

NEON DESERT

Neon Star Block

Cup and Saucer Block

Finished Quilt Size: 42" x 60"
Finished Block Size: 9" x 9"
Finished Flying Geese Segment:
  1½" x 3" for center section
  3" x 6" for outer border
Color photo: page 52

I used a print with bright colors on black to make this quilt work. I cut brightly colored areas of the black print for the centers of the Cup and Saucer blocks. Solid fabrics of intense colors were used around the center print and in the Neon Star blocks. The Flying Geese segments in the outer border are larger than the ones in the center section for design interest.

MATERIALS: 44"-wide fabric

2½ yds. of black print

2½ yds. of white

1 yd. of black solid

15 squares, each 3½" x 3½", of assorted colors to match the black print*

15 squares, each 4½" x 4½", of assorted colors to match the black print

*Use a colorful area within the black print for the block centers.

CUTTING

All measurements include ¼"-wide seam allowances.

For each Cup and Saucer block, cut:

2 squares, each 3⅞" x 3⅞", from white for corners

1 square, 4½" x 4½", from white

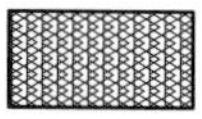

2 squares, each 3⅞" x 3⅞, from black print for corners

2 squares, each 5½" x 5½", from black print

1 square, 3½" x 3½", from black print for centers*

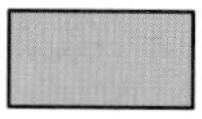

1 square, 4½" x 4½", from a solid color

*Use a colorful area within the black print for the block centers.

For each Neon Star block, cut:

2 squares, each 3⅞" x 3⅞", from white for corners

1 square, 5½" x 5½", from white

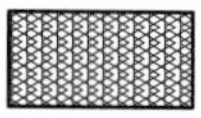

2 squares, each 3⅞" x 3⅞", from black print for corners

1 square, 4½" x 4½", from black print

1 square, 5½" x 5½", from black print

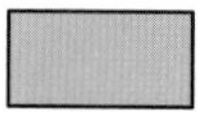

1 square, 4½" x 4½", from a solid color

1 square, 3½" x 3½", from the same solid color as above for the center of the block

DIRECTIONS

Note: To make geese segments for the blocks and borders, refer to "Flying-Geese-the-Fast-Way," beginning on page 8.

Cup and Saucer Block

1. To assemble the block corner, pair a white 3⅞" square with a black print 3⅞" square, right sides together. Mark a diagonal line, from the top left corner to the bottom right corner, on each pair as shown.

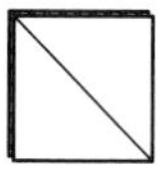

Make 2.

2. Sew ¼" away from the drawn line, along both sides as shown.

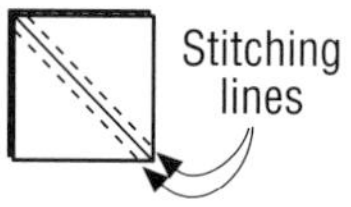

Stitching lines

3. Cut squares on the diagonal line. Open and press seam toward the darker fabric.

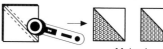

Make 4.

4. Using the 4½" and 5½" squares, make Flying Geese segments. Trim to 2" x 3½", to yield 8 segments. You will need 4 with white geese and 4 with colored geese.

Make 4.   Make 4.

5. Join each colored geese segment to a white geese segment as shown. Make 4 pairs.

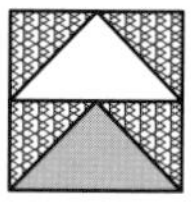

Make 4.

6. Arrange the corner units, Flying Geese segments, and center square as shown. Join the sections in rows, then join the rows to complete the block.

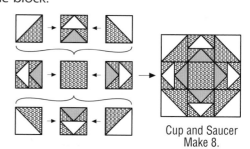

Cup and Saucer
Make 8.

Neon Star Block

1. To assemble the block corner sections, pair a white 3⅞" square with a black print 3⅞" square, right sides together. Mark a diagonal line, from the top left corner to the bottom right corner, on each pair as shown.

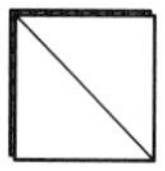

Make 2.

2. Sew ¼" away from the drawn line, along both sides as shown.

Stitching lines

3. Cut squares on the drawn diagonal line. Open and press the seam toward the dark fabric.

Make 4.

4. Using the 4½" and 5½" squares, make Flying Geese segments. Trim to 2" x 3½" to yield 8 segments. You will need 4 with black print geese and 4 with colored geese.

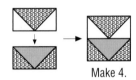

Make 4.   Make 4.

5. Join each colored geese segment to a black print geese segment as shown. Make 4 pairs.

Make 4.

6. Arrange the corner units, Flying Geese segments, and center square as shown. Join the sections in rows, then join the rows to complete the block.

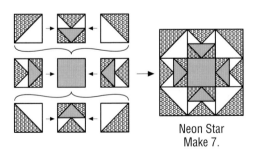

Neon Star
Make 7.

Quilt Top Assembly

1. Arrange the blocks in 5 rows of 3 blocks each, referring to the quilt plan on page 41.
2. Sew the blocks together in rows.
3. Sew the rows together.

Inner Border

This "goosed" border has ten Flying Geese segments separated by plain white strips and solid-colored corner squares.

CUTTING

All measurements include ¼"-wide seam allowances.

For the inner border, cut:
3 squares, each 4½" x 4½", from black print
3 squares, each 5½" x 5½", from white
6 strips, each 2" x 15½", from white
8 rectangles, each 2" x 3½", from white
4 squares, each 2" x 2", from a solid color

ASSEMBLY

1. Using the 4½" and 5½" squares, make Flying Geese segments. Trim to 2" x 3½", to yield 12 segments.
2. Sew the Flying Geese segments, rectangles, strips, and corner squares together as shown.

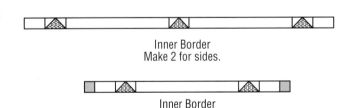

Inner Border
Make 2 for sides.

Inner Border
Make 2 for top and bottom.

3. Sew a border strip to each side of the quilt top. Sew a border strip to the top and bottom of the quilt top.

Outer Border

The outer border is made of Flying Geese segments and rectangles, with half-square triangle units in each corner. The Flying Geese segments were doubled in size in the border to give a more open feeling to the quilt top. The finished outer border geese segments measure 3" x 6".

CUTTING

All measurements include ¼"-wide seam allowances.

For the outer border, cut:
5 squares, each 7½" x 7½", from white
5 squares, each 8½" x 8½", from black solid
7 squares, each 7½" x 7½", from black print
7 squares, each 8½" x 8½", from white
4 squares, each 3⅞" x 3⅞", from white
2 squares, each 3⅞" x 3⅞", from black solid
2 squares, each 3⅞" x 3⅞", from black print
12 rectangles, each 3½" x 6½", from black solid

ASSEMBLY

1. Using the 7½" and 8½" squares, make Flying Geese segments. Trim to 3½" x 6½" to yield 48 segments. You need 20 segments with white geese, and 28 segments with black print geese.

Make 20. Make 28.

2. Sew the black print and white geese segments together in pairs as shown, with the white geese segment on top. Make 14.

Make 14.

3. Sew a black solid rectangle and a black print geese segment together as shown. Make 12.

Make 12.

4. Pair a 3⅞" white square with a 3⅞" black print square, right sides together. Repeat with a 3⅞" white square and a 3⅞" black solid square. Draw a diagonal line, from the top left corner to the bottom right corner, on each stack.

5. Sew ¼" away from the drawn line, along both sides as shown.

Stitching lines

6. Cut the squares on the diagonal line. Open and press the seam toward the darker fabric. You need 8 half-square triangle units.

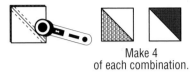

Make 4
of each combination.

7. Arrange 4 corner sections, each with 2 half-square triangle units and 1 white geese segment. You will need 2 of each arrangement as shown.

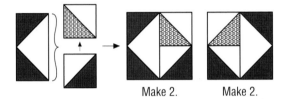

Make 2.   Make 2.

8. Join 4 Flying Geese sections with 4 rectangle/Flying Geese sections as shown for the side border. Pay careful attention to the color placement and direction of each segment. Make 2.

Outer Border
Make 2 for sides.

9. Join 3 Flying Geese sections with 2 rectangle/Flying Geese sections and 2 corner sections as shown for the top and bottom border.

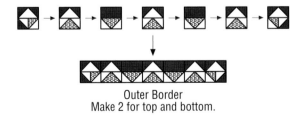

Outer Border
Make 2 for top and bottom.

10. Sew side borders to opposite sides of the quilt top, then add the top and bottom borders to complete the quilt top.

There you have it! It wasn't so difficult, was it?

Diamond Quilts

While working with my extra gaggle of geese, I found that I could make wonderful, scrappy diamond patterns quickly and easily. I allowed my leftover Flying Geese to dictate the colors and the size of my Diamond X quilt. I used every medium to dark blue and maroon fabric in my collection that was large enough to yield a 7½" square.

All of the Flying Geese segments have the same value placement: light geese and dark skies.

This quilt is made of diamond strings. Each string requires a half block at each end. Diamond strings can be set together side by side as in Diamond X, or set together with sashing strips as in the traditional Flying Geese practice piece on pages 13–15. Separate diamond strings also can be used as a very quick and interesting border treatment.

DIAMOND X

MATERIALS: 44"-wide fabric
2½ yds. of muslin
2½ yds. total of assorted dark fabrics*

* You will need 50 squares, each 7½" x 7½". The more fabrics used, the "scrappier" the quilt appears.

Make 16.

Finished Quilt Size: 55" x 65"
Finished Block Size: 10"
Finished Flying Geese Segment:
   2½" x 5"
Color photo: page 60

CUTTING

All measurements include ¼"-wide seam allowances.

From the assorted dark fabrics, cut:
46 squares, each 7½" x 7½", for the skies
10 squares, each 3⅜" x 3⅜", for half-block units

From the muslin, cut:
46 squares, each 6½" x 6½", for the geese*
4 squares, each 3" x 3", for corner half-block units
4 squares, each 3" x 3", for middle border corners
10 squares, each 3⅜" x 3⅜", for half-block units

*I cut the muslin squares along the length of the fabric so that I can cut long, unpieced border strips.

DIRECTIONS

Note: To make geese segments for blocks and borders, refer to "Flying-Geese-the-Fast-Way," beginning on page 8.

Center Section

1. Using the 7½" and 6½" squares, make Flying Geese segments. Trim to 3" x 5½" to yield 184 segments. You will need 8 Flying Geese segments for each Diamond X block.
   Make 8.

2. Arrange 8 Flying Geese segments as shown to create the X. Make the color arrangement random for a scrappy look, or plan specific color placement. It's up to you!

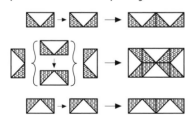

3. To assemble the corner sections, pair a 3⅜" square of dark fabric with 1 of muslin, right sides together. Mark a diagonal line, from the top left corner to the bottom right corner, on each pair as shown.

4. Sew ¼" away from the drawn line, along both sides as shown.

5. Cut squares on the diagonal line. Open and press the seam toward the darker fabric.

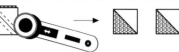

6. Assemble 4 half-block units as shown, using Flying Geese segments and half-square triangle units.

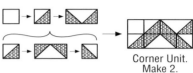
Corner Unit.
Make 2.

7. Assemble 2 corner units as shown, using Flying Geese, muslin squares, and half-square triangle units.

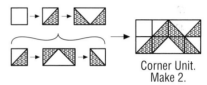
Corner Unit.
Make 2.

These corner units are for the top left and bottom right corners of the quilt top.

8. Assemble 2 corner units as shown, using Flying Geese, muslin squares, and half-square triangle units.

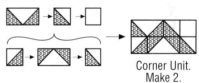
Corner Unit.
Make 2.

These corner units are for the top right and bottom left corners of the quilt top.

9. Sew the Diamond X blocks into strings of 4 blocks each, adding the correct half-block unit to each end as shown.

Left Outer
String

Inner String
Make 2.

Right Outer
String

Borders

Inner Border

All measurements include ¼"-wide seam allowances.

Cut plain border strips along the lengthwise grain to eliminate seams. To find the correct measurement for plain border strips, always measure through the center of the quilt, not at the outside edges. This ensures that the borders are of equal length on opposite sides of the quilt and brings the outer edges into line with the center dimension if discrepancies exist.

From the muslin, cut:
2 strips, each 3" x required length of the quilt top, for the sides
2 strips, each 3" x required width of the quilt top after adding the side strips, for the top and bottom

Sew a side strip to each side of the center section as shown in the quilt plan on page 46. Sew the remaining strips to the top and bottom of the quilt top.

Middle Border

1. Position the Flying Geese segments for the side borders as shown. Join the segments.

Make 2.

2. Position the Flying Geese segments for the top and bottom borders as shown. Join the segments. Add a 3" x 3" muslin square to each end of the top and bottom strips.

Make 2.

Outer Border

See cutting directions for plain inner border at left.

From the muslin, cut:
2 strips, each 3" x required length of the quilt top, for the side border
2 strips, each 3" x required width of the quilt top after adding the side borders, for the top and bottom border

Add the plain outer border strips as shown for the plain inner border.

There it is! An easy, interesting scrap quilt with no templates to trace.

Gallery of Quilts

Spring Mosaic by Mary Sue Suit, 1993, Alliance, Nebraska, 68" x 84".
Two of the easiest quilt blocks combine for a seemingly complex design.

Geese and Squares by Mary Sue Suit, 1993, Alliance, Nebraska, 36" x 36". Pairs of geese and squares make up this high-flying practice project. If made larger, this could be a striking bed-size quilt.

Pinkie by Mary Sue Suit, 1993, Alliance, Nebraska, 38" x 38". Sunset shades of mauve and pink highlight this Geese-and-Squares flight of fancy.

Aunt Sukey's Choice by Mary Sue Suit, 1993, Alliance, Nebraska, 48" x 60".
Mary Sue used her fast method to make the Flying Geese and
repeated a traditional block to create this wonderful quilt.
Quilted by Mary Lucas, Littleton, Colorado (Thanks, Mom).

Neon Desert by Mary Sue Suit, 1993,
Alliance, Nebraska, 42" x 60".
Intense colors and a bold print
light up this two-block quilt.

Homage to M. C. Escher by Pegee Haman,
1993, Billings, Montana, 26" x 27".
Sophisticated color and arrangement is
reminiscent of artist M. C. Escher.

Dutchman's Puzzle by Yvonne Morrisey,
1993, Silesia, Montana, 46" x 71".
This repeat-block quilt, combining pinks
and teals, is easy to make.

Flying Elephants by Barbara Olson,
1993, Billings, Montana, 49" x 41".
The geese got lost and an
elephant took over.

All the Blocks are Geese Sampler by Mary Sue Suit, 1992, Alliance, Nebraska, 56" x 70".
This sampler of traditional blocks is quick and easy to make, using the
Flying-Geese-the-Fast-Way technique and a few new tricks.

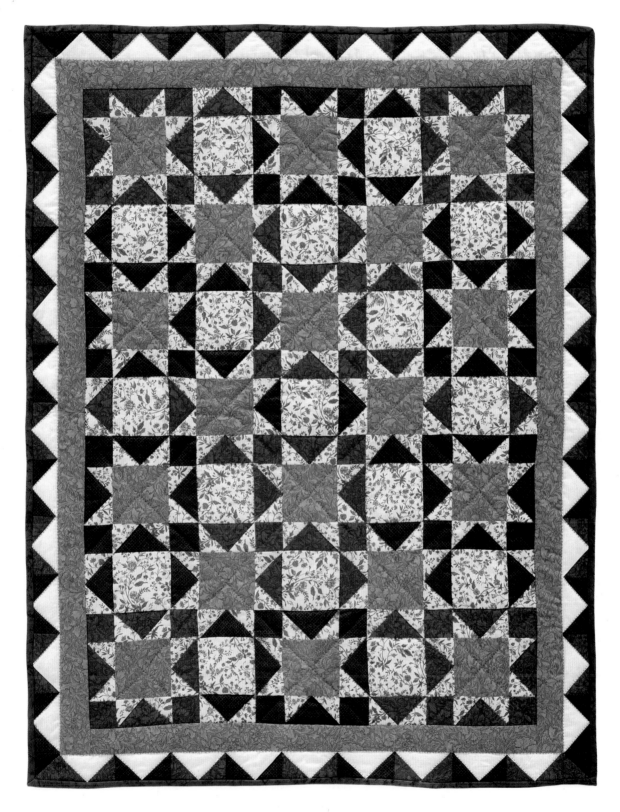

Evening Star Repeat by Mary Sue Suit, 1993, Alliance, Nebraska, 30" x 38". This quilt shows how the repeat of a simple block set together with a Flying Geese sashing takes on a complex appearance.

Bright Star by Mary Sue Suit, 1992, Alliance, Nebraska, 40" x 40". The author had fun with a charm packet of solid fabrics for her first flight of fancy.

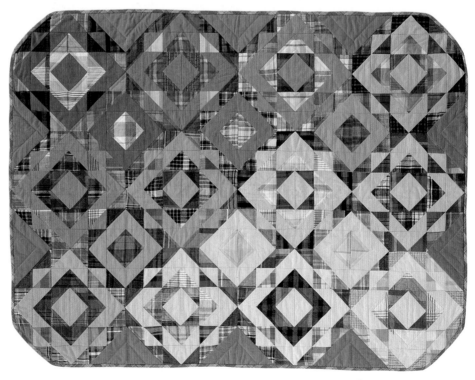

Madras Geese by Lyn Banks, 1993, Billings, Montana, 49" x 37". Flying Geese East has a spicy look of India.

Goose Flight by Mary Sue Suit, 1984, Alliance, Nebraska, 48" x 48". After tracing all the triangles for this contemporary quilt, the author refused to make any more Flying Geese until she discovered her quick-geese technique.

Whirling Geese by Margie Hay, 1993, Billings, Montana, 32" x 32". Like carnival rides, these colorful geese appear to go 'round and 'round.

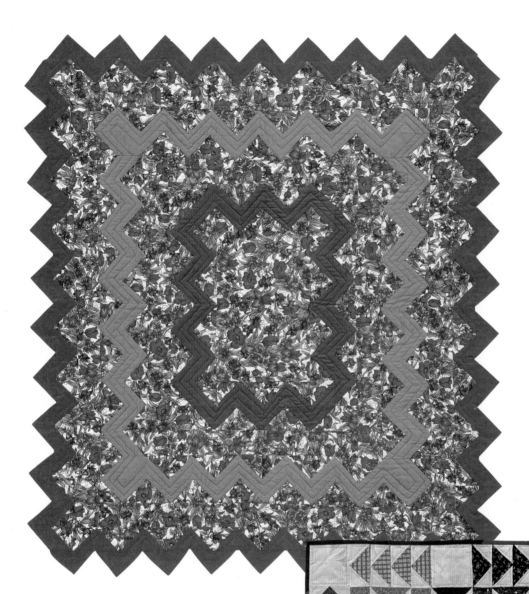

Rick-Rack by Judy Harris, 1993, Livingston, Montana, 39" x 42½". The zigzag design extends to the quilt edge and is finished with prairie points.

Christmas Geese by Mary Sue Suit, 1993, Alliance, Nebraska, 28" x 28". Evening Star blocks and Flying Geese sashing make a stunning secondary pattern. This would also make an easy, attractive scrap quilt.

Mary Ellen's Gaggle by Mary Ellen Reynolds, 1993, Alliance, Nebraska, 68" x 68".
Teamed with solid blocks to show off quilting stitches, this is a sampler with a difference.

Diamond X by Mary Sue Suit, 1993, Alliance, Nebraska, 55" x 65".
This fast, easy quilt is a great way to use up some of your scraps.

Karen's Geese by Karen Walker, 1993, Lakeside, Nebraska, 48" x 60".
Karen's sampler quilt was her first attempt at machine piecing.

Flying Geese Jacket by Mary Sue Suit, 1992, Alliance, Nebraska. Made from 100% wool, this jacket is a pleasure to piece and wonderful to wear.

Amish Geese by Dorothy Bull, 1992, Alliance, Nebraska, 26" x 36". Black and solid colors give this flight of fancy an Amish flavor.

Nebraska Windmill Scene by Dorothy Bull, 1992, Alliance, Nebraska, 40" x 60". The Flying Geese border makes a perfect frame and carries the motion of the windmill to the edges of the wall hanging.

Nebraska 125 by Mary Sue Suit, 1992, Alliance, Nebraska, 42" x 60". Mary Sue invented her Flying-Geese-the-Fast-Way technique to make the border on this quilt.

Flying Geese by Mary Sue Suit, 1993, Alliance, Nebraska, 32" x 40". This practice project uses the traditional straight-row set of Flying Geese along with a Flying Geese border.

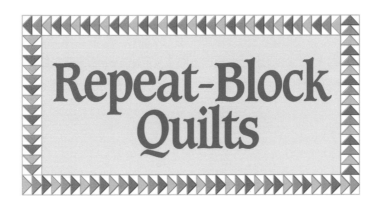

Repeat-Block Quilts

The easiest quilt tops to make are those that repeat one block the required number of times. The quilt below is made of twelve Aunt Sukey's Choice blocks. The 12" blocks are pieced exactly like the Aunt Sukey's Choice block in the sampler quilt on pages 25–26. The outer border is made of Flying Geese segments.

The outer Flying Geese border and the sashing add 12" to the length and width of the quilt top, making it easy to increase the size. For example, twenty blocks, set in rows of 4 blocks across by 5 blocks down, with the same border, would measure 60" x 72". Thirty blocks, set in rows of 5 blocks across by 6 blocks down, with the same border would measure 72" x 84".

Aunt Sukey's Choice

Note: If you used templates and cut pieces for this quilt the traditional way, you would cut 576 triangles. With this method, you cut only 96 squares.

MATERIALS: 44"-WIDE FABRIC
1½ yds. print fabric for 12 block centers , 24 squares for geese and inner border strips
2 yds. muslin for geese, skies, and corner sections
1 yd. solid fabric for skies and corner squares* OR ¼ yd. each of 12 assorted fabrics*
3 yds. for backing
¾ yd. for binding
54" x 65" piece of batting

*If you are using scraps, you will need a piece large enough to cut a 6½" x 6½" square.

Finished Quilt Size: 48" x 60"
Finished Block Size: 12" x 12"
Finished Flying Geese Segment: 2" x 4"
Color photo: page 51

Aunt Sukey's Choice Blocks

CUTTING
All measurements include ¼"-wide seam allowances.

From print Fabric A, cut:
12 squares, each 5½" x 5½", for geese*
12 squares, each 4½" x 4½", for centers*

*Because I prefer not to piece the inner border strips, I usually cut the squares down the length of the fabric. This ensures enough fabric for the long border strips.

From muslin, cut:
12 squares, each 5½" x 5½", for geese
12 squares, each 6½" x 6½", for skies
12 squares, each 5" x 5", for corners
24 rectangles, each 4½" x 5", for corners

From solid Fabric B and/or assorted fabric, cut:
12 squares, each 6½" x 6½", for skies
12 squares, each 5" x 5", for corners

DIRECTIONS
Note: To make geese segments for blocks and borders, refer to "Flying-Geese-the-Fast-Way," beginning on page 8.

1. Using the 6½" and 7½" squares, make Flying Geese segments. For color placement, see Aunt Sukey's Choice sampler block on pages 25–26.

2. Sew a Fabric A, print geese segment to the top edge of a Fabric B, muslin geese segment as shown. Make 4.

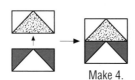
Make 4.

3. To assemble the corner sections, mark the center of two 5" squares by folding them in half and lightly pressing the fold.

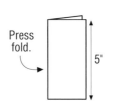
Press fold.
5"

4. Stack the squares right sides together, matching center folds. Sew along both sides of the center fold, ¼" away from the fold.

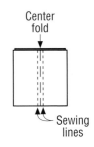
Center fold
Sewing lines

5. Cut on the fold line, open the squares, and press the seams toward the darker fabric.

6. Center a square unit on top of a 4½" x 5" rectangle, right sides together, as shown. Draw a vertical line at the 2½" center point.

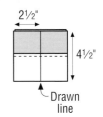
2½"
4½"
Drawn line

7. Sew ¼" away from the drawn line, along both sides as shown.

Stitching lines

8. Cut apart along the drawn line. Open and press.

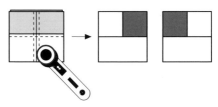

9. Arrange the Flying Geese, the print center square, and corner sections as shown below. Join sections to complete the block. Make 12.

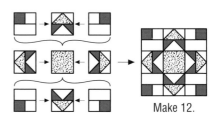
Make 12.

10. Arrange blocks in 4 rows of 3 blocks each.

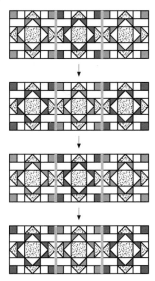

11. Join the rows to complete the quilt top.

Borders

To find the correct measurement for the plain inner border strips, always measure through the center of the quilt, not at the outside edges. This ensures that the borders are of equal length on opposite sides of the quilt and brings the outer edges into line with the center dimension if discrepancies exist.

Repeat-block quilts can also be assembled with sashing between the blocks as in the sampler quilt on page 20. You may want to add Flying Geese segments to the sashing between the blocks. If you do, a secondary pattern will emerge. The Evening Star repeat-block quilt shown on page 55 and the Christmas Geese quilt on page 58 are both set together with Flying Geese sashing.

Be creative. Let your imagination go and see what happens.

CUTTING

All measurements include ¼"-wide seam allowances.

From the muslin, cut:
12 squares, each 6½" x 6½", for border skies
12 squares, each 5½" x 5½", for border Flying Geese
1 square, 5" x 5", for corner
2 rectangles, each 4½" x 5"

From the print fabric, cut:
2 strips, each 2½" x the center length of the quilt plus ½", for the inner side borders
2 strips, each 2½" x the center width of the quilt plus side borders and ½" for inner top and bottom border seam allowances
12 squares, each 5½" x 5½", for border Flying Geese

From the coordinating fabrics, cut:
12 squares, each 6½" x 6½", for border skies*
1 square, 5" x 5", for corner

*I used 12 different coordinating fabrics, so I cut 1 square from each.

DIRECTIONS

1. Sew a plain border strip to each side of the quilt top. Press seams toward the border. Sew a plain border strip to the top and bottom of the quilt top. Press seams toward the border.

2. To make the Flying Geese segments for the pieced border, use the 5½" and 6½" squares. Trim to 2½" x 4½", to yield 96 Flying Geese segments.

3. Sew the segments together in pairs to make 48 sections as shown.

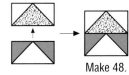

Make 48.

4. To assemble the corner sections, mark the center of two 5" x 5" squares by folding them in half and lightly pressing the fold.

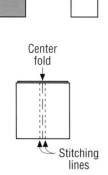

Press fold.

Center fold

5. Stack the squares right sides together, matching center folds. Sew along both sides of the center fold, ¼" away from the fold.

Stitching lines

6. Cut on the fold line, open the squares, and press the seams toward the darker fabric.

7. Center a square unit on top of a 4½" x 5" rectangle, right sides together, as shown. Draw a vertical line at the 2½" center point.

Drawn ine

8. Sew ¼" away from the drawn line, along both sides as shown.

Stitching lines

Cut apart along the drawn line. Open and press.

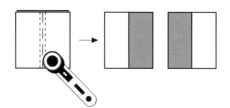

Make 4.

9. Assemble the side pieced border strips, using 13 Flying Geese segments.

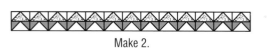

Make 2.

10. Sew a pieced outer border strip to each side of the quilt top.

11. Assemble the top and bottom pieced border strips, using 10 Flying Geese segments.

Make 2.

12. Sew a corner section to each end of the top and bottom pieced border strips.

Top border

Bottom border

Sew the completed top and bottom pieced border strips to the quilt.

13. Finish your Aunt Sukey's Choice quilt, following the directions on pages 77–79.

Borders

The most delightful and unexpected use of the Flying Geese segments has been the easy, effective borders I have been able to make. Look through the photographs on pages 49–64 to find all the borders that consist of Flying Geese segments. These segments can be used for quilt borders, surrounding blocks made from Flying Geese segments, or as frames around other quilt blocks. Notice how the use of Flying Geese segments carries the design to the edge of the quilt in Dorothy Bull's "Nebraska Windmill Scene" on page 63. This technique was developed when I made the "Nebraska 125" wall hanging on page 63. I was determined to use Flying Geese as a border, but I refused to trace triangles. I guess I should be happy I am so stubborn or lazy—I'm not sure which! The wall hanging, "Goose Flight," was pieced almost ten years ago the "old way"— I was young and foolish. I swore off Flying Geese after that border, until now.

Thoughts About Borders

▲ To string the Flying Geese segments end to end, you must be able to evenly divide the length and width measurement of the quilt top by the same number.

▲ You need an odd number of Flying Geese segments for all the corners to look the same. Or, you can design from the corners to the center and adjust the color or change the geese direction at the midpoint of the borders as pictured on page 70.

▲ When constructing borders by piecing the segments end to end, cut the border corner squares the same size as the height of the Flying Geese segment.

▲ When adding plain border strips to the quilt top, make the width of the plain strips equal to the height of the Flying Geese segment in the pieced section. This adds a whole segment width to the length and width of the quilt.

▲ When making borders of two Flying Geese segments, cut the corner squares the same size as the two Flying Geese pieced segments used in the border.

▲ A rectangle used in a double border treatment measures the same size as the Flying Geese segment.

TRADITIONAL

The following shows a very traditional way of using Flying Geese in a border. Several corner variations are also shown below.

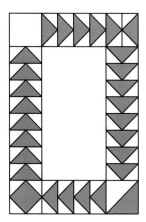

This traditional border treatment shows the geese flying in both directions on each side of the border, and several corner and center variations.

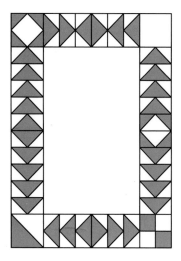

END-TO-END

Single Geese

Options for easy border treatments, using single Flying Geese segments, are shown below. The corners of each border round show some variations.

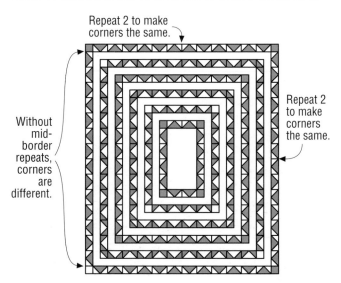

Double Flying Geese

These borders are made with two Flying Geese segments or a single segment and a rectangle. More corner variations are shown.

I am certain of one thing. There are many more Flying Geese border designs out there. Just when I think I have found them all, another one presents itself. So, have fun and find some new ones!

Block Glossary

This Flying Geese technique is very useful in piecing a great many traditional blocks. The directions for other piecing tricks used in these blocks are in the Sampler chapter on pages 20–34.

The blocks in this book are composed on grids of equal squares as if drawn on graph paper. It is easy to adjust the block size and to determine the correct size of the squares of fabric needed to piece the block by using the formulas below. Divide the size of the block by the number of equal squares in one row of the block. This equals the size of one grid square. Some segments of the block may cover more than one grid square. The center segment of the block often covers four grid squares. Remember, the Flying Geese segment covers either two grid squares, or two Flying Geese segments cover one grid square.

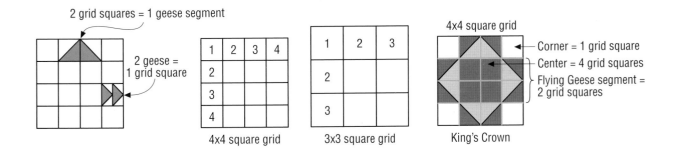

Grid Formulas

Calculating measurements of squares for geese and sky:

> Desired width of Flying Geese segment + 1½"
>   = geese square
> Dimension of geese square + 1" = sky square

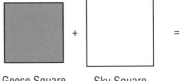

Calculating measurements of half-square triangle units:

> Desired finished square + ⅞". See page 27, steps 3 and 4, for directions on how to assemble these units.

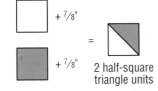

Calculating measurements of a pieced rectangle:

This segment usually covers 2 grid squares.

3 x the grid square + 1" = rectangle length

grid square + $\frac{1}{2}$" = rectangle width

grid square + $1\frac{1}{2}$" = square

1 square + 1 rectangle yields 2 segments

Any added triangle will need to be trimmed. Make sure the correct dimensions fall where the fabrics intersect. See the directions for the Seesaw block or the Next-Door Neighbor block in the Sampler chapter on pages 21–23 for the assembly technique.

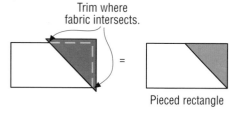

Trim where fabric intersects.

Pieced rectangle

Calculating measurements for Aunt Sukey's Corner:

For all 4 corners containing 4 different fabrics, use 2 squares and 2 rectangles. This technique makes 4 corner sections from 2 squares and 2 rectangles. See Aunt Sukey's Choice block, beginning on page 25.

Finished corner size + 1" = squares (one of each color)

Square size x corner size + $\frac{1}{2}$" = rectangles, 2 of same color

2 squares + 2 rectangles yields 4 units

Aunt Sukey's Choice corner

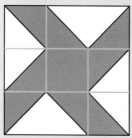

Box
2 Flying Geese
4 half-square triangle units
1 square

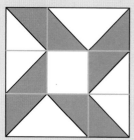

Formal Garden
4 Flying Geese
1 square

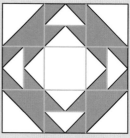

Cup and Saucer
8 Flying Geese
4 half-square triangle units
1 square

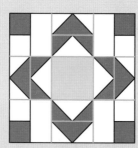

Aunt Sukey's Choice
8 Flying Geese
4 corner units
1 square

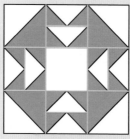

Capital T
8 Flying Geese
4 half-square triangle units
1 square

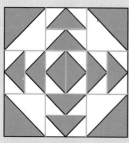

Illinois
10 Flying Geese
4 half-square triangle units

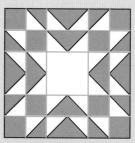

Star Gardener
8 Flying Geese
8 half-square triangle units
1 large square
8 small squares

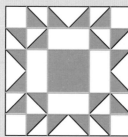

Arizona
4 Flying Geese
12 half-square triangle units
4 rectangles
1 large square
4 small squares

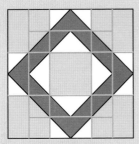

Wyoming Valley
10 Flying Geese
12 half-square triangle units
4 squares

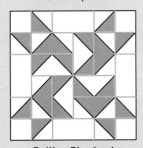

Ninepatch Frame
8 Flying Geese
4 half-square triangle units
4 rectangles
1 large square
4 small squares

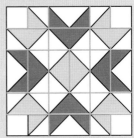

Swing in the Center
14 Flying Geese
4 half-square triangle units
4 squares

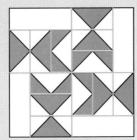

Flying Dutchman
12 Flying Geese
4 rectangles

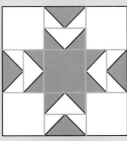

Eight-Pointed Star
8 Flying Geese
5 squares

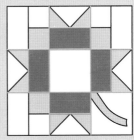

Rolling Pinwheel
8 Flying Geese
8 half-square triangle units
4 squares
4 rectangles

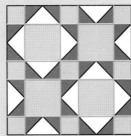

Maple Leaf
4 Flying Geese
3 corner units
2 squares
4 rectangles
1 appliqué stem

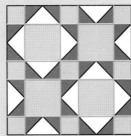

Road to California
12 Flying Geese
4 large squares
9 small squares

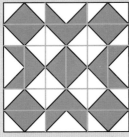

Swing in the Center II
18 Flying Geese

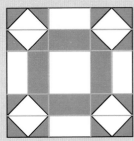

Single Wedding Ring
8 Flying Geese
1 square
8 rectangles

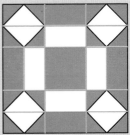

Rolling Stone
8 Flying Geese
1 square
8 rectangles

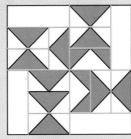

Ladies' Wreath
12 Flying Geese
4 rectangles

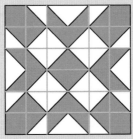

Dumbell Block
14 Flying Geese
4 half-square triangle units
4 squares

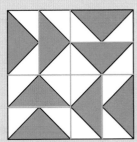

Mosaic
8 Flying Geese

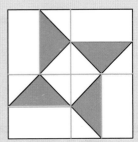

Pinwheel Askew
4 Flying Geese
4 rectangles

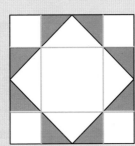

Art Square
4 Flying Geese
1 large square
4 small squares

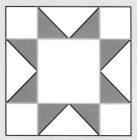

Evening Star
4 Flying Geese
1 large square
4 small squares

Stars and Squares
8 Flying Geese
4 large squares
1 medium square
4 small squares

Eight Hands Around
8 Flying Geese
4 half-square triangle units
1 large square
4 small squares

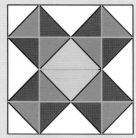

Tippecanoe and Tyler Too
6 Flying Geese
4 half-square triangle units

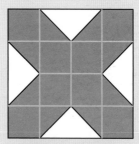

Mother's Choice I
4 Flying Geese
8 squares

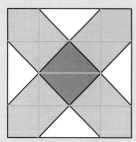

Pointed Tile
6 Flying Geese
4 squares

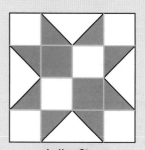

Indian Star
4 Flying Geese
8 squares

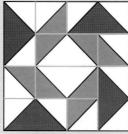

Balkan Puzzle
6 Flying Geese
4 half-square triangle units

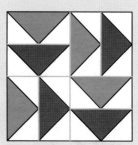

Return of the Swallows
8 Flying Geese

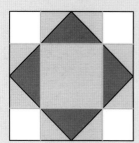

Album II
4 Flying Geese
1 large square
4 small squares

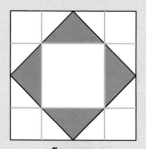

Economy
4 Flying Geese
1 large square
4 small squares

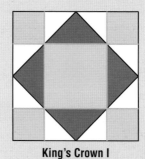

King's Crown I
4 Flying Geese
1 large square
4 small squares

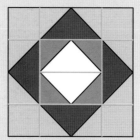

Twelve Triangles
6 Flying Geese
4 squares

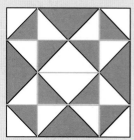

Star II
6 Flying Geese
4 half-square triangle units

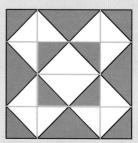

Star III
6 Flying Geese
4 half-square triangle units

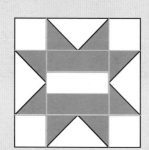

Album Star
4 Flying Geese
4 squares
3 rectangles

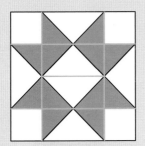

Ribbon Star
6 Flying Geese
1 large square
4 small squares

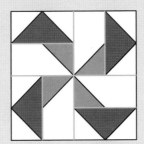

Seesaw
4 Flying Geese
4 pieced rectangle units

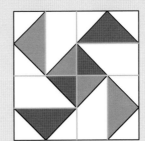

Next-Door Neighbor
4 Flying Geese
4 pieced rectangle units

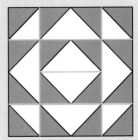

Mosaic II
6 Flying Geese
4 half-square triangle units

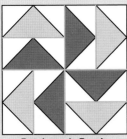

Dutchman's Puzzle
8 Flying Geese

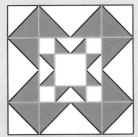

Eight Hands All Around II
8 Flying Geese
4 half-square triangle units
1 large square
4 small squares

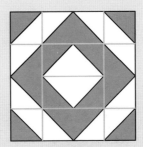

Fancy Stripe
6 Flying Geese
4 half-square triangle units

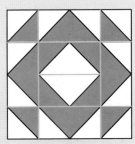

Broken Dishes II
6 Flying Geese
4 half-square triangle units

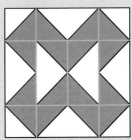

Hourglass II
6 Flying Geese
4 half-square triangle units

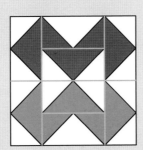

Double Z
8 Flying Geese

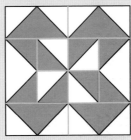

Colorado Block
6 Flying Geese
4 half-sqaure triangle units

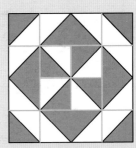

Pinwheel III
4 Flying Geese
8 half-square triangle units

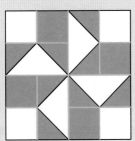

Pinwheel IV
4 Flying Geese
8 squares

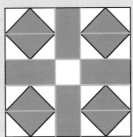

Garden of Eden
8 Flying Geese
1 square
4 rectangles

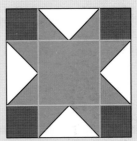

Arrow Star
4 Flying Geese
5 squares

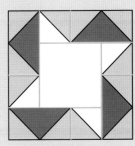

July 4th
4 Flying Geese
4 half-square triangle units
1 square

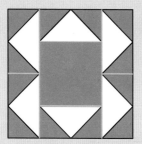

Buzzard's Roost
6 Flying Geese
1 square

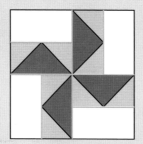

Louisiana
4 Flying Geese
4 rectangles

Yankee Puzzle
4 Flying Geese
8 half-square triangle units

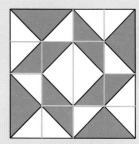

Whirlpool
6 Flying Geese
4 half-square triangle units

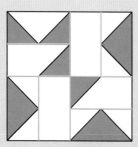

Blockade
4 Flying Geese
2 pieced rectangle units
2 rectangles

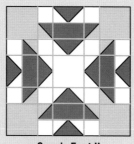

Crow's Foot II
8 Flying Geese
8 half-square triangle units
16 squares

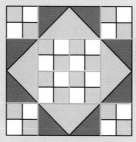

Road to California II
4 Flying Geese
8 four-patch units

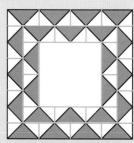

Our Village Green
24 Flying Geese
1 square

Odd Fellow's Chain
12 Flying Geese
8 half-square triangle units
12 squares
8 pieced rectangle units

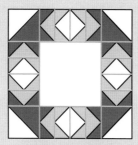

Cupid's Arrow Point
16 Flying Geese
4 half-square triangle units
1 square

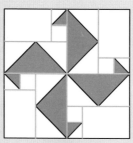

Lindy's Plane
4 Flying Geese
4 half-square triangle units
4 squares
4 rectangles

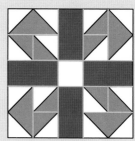

Jack in the Box
4 Flying Geese
8 half-square triangle units
1 square
4 rectangles

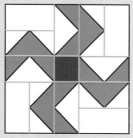

Kicks
8 Flying Geese
1 square
4 rectangles

Finishing Your Quilt

Now that you have a beautiful quilt top, it is important to remember that it isn't a quilt until it's quilted! No matter how perfect the colors and piecing are, it won't be an heirloom quilt if it isn't finished. The highest status it can achieve is that of heirloom top or a work in progress. If your quilt top is not your heart's desire, it can be tied or machine quilted. (You may not wish to invest the time to hand quilt it.) I love hand quilting, so I will quilt almost anything.

I am only an expert on how I do things. There are many fine resources available on quilt finishing techniques, including books, quilt classes, and knowledgeable quilt-shop personnel.

Here is how I finish a quilt:

Press the quilt top. After lots of trial and error, I finally learned the value of pressing the quilt top before layering and basting it. (Hi, Mom! She always told me so.) Before I even think about assembling the layers, I give the quilt top one last press and check the back for any long threads that need to be trimmed. I also make sure no dark threads are long enough to show through a lighter section. If it sounds like I learned this from experience, you are right. I have probably done every dumb thing you can think of because I was in a hurry to finish a quilt.

Mark the quilting pattern. Most quilters mark the quilting pattern on the quilt top before basting the layers together. This is especially important if you quilt on a frame or with a group. However, I quilt on a hoop and mark as I go. If the fabric is light enough, I prefer a very sharp, hard lead pencil for marking. Mark as lightly as possible. Water-soluble quilt marking pens are available, but I have had difficulty removing the marks, and quite often, the one pen I have has dried out. When you live in the "outback," it is not always possible to run out to buy a new one when you need it.

Pink, yellow, and white pencils work well for marking dark fabrics. Because I usually mark as I go, I often use soap slivers to mark dark fabrics. Save the little pieces of soap that haunt the bathroom and let them dry out. It works best if the sliver is thin and hard. Avoid using moisturizing bars as they may be oily. Soap helps the needle slide through the fabric and has usually disappeared by the time you have finished the quilting. If not, the soap marks wipe off with a damp cloth.

Quilting straight lines is easier with the use of ¼"-wide masking tape. It is usually available in quilt shops and supply catalogs. It is best to position the tape as you quilt rather than taping the entire top at once. The tape can be difficult to remove when left in place too long, and it may leave a residue. Besides, you can usually use one piece of tape several times before discarding it.

Baste. This is another step I grew into the hard way. If you quilt in a hoop as I do, rather than a frame, it is doubly important to baste the quilt "sandwich" generously. Those who quilt on a frame also agree that basting is an important step.

To baste your quilt:

Lay the backing fabric, wrong side up, on a flat surface. I use the living-room floor. Smooth out all the wrinkles. I allow extra backing fabric when hoop quilting, at least 2" on each side.

Spread the batting on top of the backing fabric, making sure it is lying flat. Some batting benefits from "breathing" or "relaxing" after it has been opened out, before basting.

Lay the pressed quilt top, right side up, on top of the other two layers. Smooth out any wrinkles, making sure all three layers are flat.

Using light-colored thread and long basting stitches, baste from the center of the quilt out to each corner. Fill in the remaining areas with basting rows spaced 4"–6" apart.

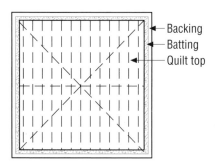

Backing
Batting
Quilt top

Because I quilt on a hoop, the quilt sandwich gets manhandled quite a bit. To protect the outside edges of the top and batting, I bring the excess backing around to the front and baste in place. This keeps the top edges from being frayed and the batting from being pulled until I am ready to quilt those areas.

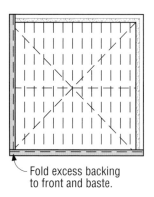

Fold excess backing to front and baste.

Once basted, the quilt sandwich is ready for quilting. This is the best part of the whole process for me. It took awhile for that to be so, but now I think there can never be too much quilting on a project. Don't be discouraged if your first stitches seem a little long. If you start quilting in the middle of the quilt, by the time you reach the edges they will be much smaller. For hand-quilting instruc-

tions, I recommend Loving Stitches by Jeana Kimball, or you can take a hand-quilting class.

When the quilting is completed, add the binding. The binding can be cut on the straight of grain or on the bias. I prefer bias binding because it wears better. As a rule, allow ½ yard of fabric to bind a crib or wall-size quilt, ¾ yard for a twin, 1 yard for a double or queen, and 1¼ yards for a king-size quilt.

To bind your quilt:

Cut the binding fabric into bias strips 2½" wide.

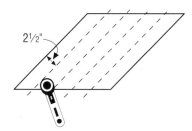

2½"

Sew the bias strips, right sides together, to make one long bias strip. Press the seams open.

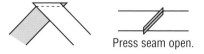

Press seam open.

Fold the strip in half lengthwise, wrong sides together, and press.

Fold line

I include a step most others feel is unnecessary. I do not know if it is just me, or my machine, but I often have pulls and ripples between the last quilted row and the binding. I add a line of basting through all three layers, at the outer edges of the quilt top, making sure everything is flat and smooth before trimming off the excess batting and backing. Since adding this step, I have found that my binding is smoother and most of the rippling is gone.

Unfold one end of the binding and turn under ¼". Starting in the center on one side of the quilt, stitch the binding to the quilt with the raw edges of the binding even with the edges of the quilt top. I use a ⅜"-wide seam allowance. Stitch to within

⅜" of the corner. Backstitch and remove the quilt from the machine. Turn the top so you are ready to stitch the next side. To miter the corner, fold the binding up as shown to form a 45° fold.

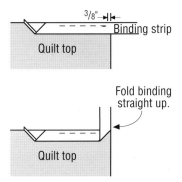

Fold the binding down, keeping the fold even with the top edge of the quilt and the raw edges of the binding even with the side edge of the quilt. Pin the pleat formed at the fold in place. Stitch, ending the stitching ⅜" away from the next corner. Repeat the process for the remaining sides.

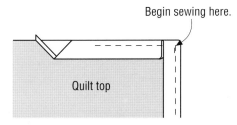

When you reach the beginning of the binding, cut the binding 1" longer than needed and tuck the end inside the beginning of the strip. Fold the binding over the raw edges of the quilt and blindstitch in place on the back of the quilt. The corners will automatically form miters as you turn them. Sew the miters in place.

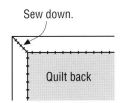

Breathe a huge sigh of relief. The quilt is finished!

Meet the author

Mary Sue Suit lives with her family — 1 husband, 2 kids, 1 dog, 1 cat, and a station wagon — in western Nebraska. A self-taught quilter, Mary Sue has been quilting for about fifteen years and is always looking for the quickest way to do things. While living in Montana, she was a member of several quilt groups and taught classes in Billings and the surrounding area. Her work has been included in shows at the Castle Art Gallery and the Yellowstone Exhibition. She is an active member of the Panhandle Quilt Guild.

That Patchwork Place Publications and Products

BOOKS

All the Blocks Are Geese by Mary Sue Suit
Angle Antics by Mary Hickey
Animas Quilts by Jackie Robinson
Appliqué Borders: An Added Grace by Jeana Kimball
Appliquilt™: Whimsical One-Step Appliqué by Tonee White
Baltimore Bouquets by Mimi Dietrich
Basket Garden by Mary Hickey
Biblical Blocks by Rosemary Makhan
Blockbuster Quilts by Margaret J. Miller
Calendar Quilts by Joan Hanson
Cathedral Window: A Fresh Look by Nancy J. Martin
Corners in the Cabin by Paulette Peters
Country Medallion Sampler by Carol Doak
Country Threads by Connie Tesene and Mary Tendall
Easy Machine Paper Piecing by Carol Doak
Even More by Trudie Hughes
Fantasy Flowers: Pieced Flowers for Quilters
    by Doreen Cronkite Burbank
Fit To Be Tied by Judy Hopkins
Five- and Seven-Patch Blocks & Quilts for the ScrapSaver™
    by Judy Hopkins
Four-Patch Blocks & Quilts for the ScrapSaver™
    by Judy Hopkins
Fun with Fat Quarters by Nancy J. Martin
Go Wild with Quilts: 14 North American Birds and Animals
    by Margaret Rolfe
Handmade Quilts by Mimi Dietrich
Happy Endings—Finishing the Edges of Your Quilt
    by Mimi Dietrich
Holiday Happenings by Christal Carter
Home for Christmas by Nancy J. Martin and Sharon Stanley
In The Beginning by Sharon Evans Yenter
Jacket Jazz by Judy Murrah
Lessons in Machine Piecing by Marsha McCloskey
Little By Little: Quilts in Miniature by Mary Hickey
Little Quilts by Alice Berg, Sylvia Johnson, and
    Mary Ellen Von Holt
Lively Little Logs by Donna McConnell
Loving Stitches: A Guide to Fine Hand Quilting
    by Jeana Kimball
More Template-Free™ Quiltmaking by Trudie Hughes
Nifty Ninepatches by Carolann M. Palmer
Nine-Patch Blocks & Quilts for the ScrapSaver™
    by Judy Hopkins
Not Just Quilts by Jo Parrott
On to Square Two by Marsha McCloskey
Osage County Quilt Factory by Virginia Robertson
Painless Borders by Sally Schneider
A Perfect Match: A Guide to Precise Machine Piecing
    by Donna Lynn Thomas
Picture Perfect Patchwork by Naomi Norman
Piecemakers® Country Store by the Piecemakers
Pineapple Passion by Nancy Smith and Lynda Milligan

A Pioneer Doll and Her Quilts by Mary Hickey
Pioneer Storybook Quilts by Mary Hickey
Prairie People—Cloth Dolls to Make and Cherish by Marji
    Hadley and J. Dianne Ridgley
*Quick & Easy Quiltmaking: 26 Projects Featuring Speedy
    Cutting and Piecing Methods* by Mary Hickey,
    Nancy J. Martin, Marsha McCloskey & Sara Nephew
*The Quilters' Companion: Everything You Need to Know to
    Make Beautiful Quilts* compiled by That Patchwork Place
Quilted for Christmas compiled by Ursula Reikes
Quilts for All Seasons: Year-Round Log Cabin Designs
    by Christal Carter
Quilts for Baby: Easy as A, B, C by Ursula Reikes
Quilts for Kids by Carolann M. Palmer
Quilts from Nature by Joan Colvin
Quilts to Share by Janet Kime
Red and Green: An Appliqué Tradition by Jeana Kimball
Red Wagon Originals by Gerry Kimmel and Linda Brannock
Rotary Riot: 40 Fast & Fabulous Quilts by Judy Hopkins
    and Nancy J. Martin
Rotary Roundup: 40 More Fast & Fabulous Quilts by Judy
    Hopkins and Nancy J. Martin
Round About Quilts by J. Michelle Watts
Samplings from the Sea by Rosemary Makhan
Scrap Happy by Sally Schneider
ScrapMania by Sally Schneider
*Sensational Settings: Over 80 Ways to Arrange Your Quilt
    Blocks* by Joan Hanson
Sewing on the Line: Fast and Easy Foundation Piecing
    by Lesly-Claire Greenberg
Shortcuts: A Concise Guide to Rotary Cutting
    by Donna Lynn Thomas (metric version available)
Shortcuts Sampler by Roxanne Carter
Shortcuts to the Top by Donna Lynn Thomas
Small Talk by Donna Lynn Thomas
Smoothstitch™ Quilts: Easy Machine Appliqué
    by Roxi Eppler
The Stitchin' Post by Jean Wells and Lawry Thorn
Strips That Sizzle by Margaret J. Miller
Tea Party Time: Romantic Quilts and Tasty Tidbits
    by Nancy J. Martin
Template-Free™ Quiltmaking by Trudie Hughes
Template-Free™ Quilts and Borders by Trudie Hughes
Template-Free® Stars by Jo Parrott
Watercolor Quilts by Pat Maixner Magaret and
    Donna Ingram Slusser
Women and Their Quilts by Nancyann Johanson Twelker

TOOLS

6" Bias Square®   BiRangle™   Rotary Rule™
8" Bias Square®   Pineapple Rule   Ruby Beholder™
Metric Bias Square®   Rotary Mate™   ScrapSaver™

VIDEO

Shortcuts to America's Best-Loved Quilts

Many titles are available at your local quilt shop. For more information, send $2 for a color
catalog to That Patchwork Place, Inc., PO Box 118, Bothell WA 98041-0118 USA.

☎ Call 1-800-426-3126 for the name and location of the quilt shop nearest you.